# Passport *to* Learning

## Teaching Social Studies to ESL Students

W9-ABZ-611

Bárbara C. Cruz

Joyce W. Nutta

Jason O'Brien

Carine M. Feyten

Jane M. Govoni

BOWLING GREEN STATE
UNIVERSITY LIBRARIES

**NCSS**

# NCSS BULLETIN 101

# National Council for the Social Studies

8555 SIXTEENTH STREET ▸ SUITE 500 ▸ SILVER SPRING, MARYLAND 20910
301 588-1800  FAX 301 588-2049  WWW.SOCIALSTUDIES.ORG

**Board of Directors**

Stephen Johnson
*President*

Denee Mattioli
*President-Elect*

Jesus Garcia
*Vice President*

Susan Adler
Peggy Altoff
William Amburn
Phyllis Bowie
Joseph A. Braun, Jr.
Susie Burroughs
Adrian Davis
L. Jill Ehlen
Mark Finchum
Betsy Fitzgerald
Debbie Gallagher
Ken Mareski
Merry Merryfield
Judy Parsons
Christine Pratt-Consoletti
Lynda Wagner
Bruce Wendt
Michael M. Yell
Ruben Zepeda

**Ex Officio**

Steven Goldberg
*House of Delegates*
*Steering Committee Chair*

Dean Cantu
*Publications Committee Chair*
*2002-2003*

**Executive Director**
Susan Griffin

**Department Directors**
Timothy Daly
*Administration*

Al Frascella
*Communications/Govt. Relations*

Arthur Ganta
*Finance*

Ella McDowell
*Meetings*

Cassandra Roberts
*Membership Processing*

Michael Simpson
*Publications*

Editorial Staff on this Publication: Jennifer Bauduy, Steven S. Lapham, Michael Simpson
Art Director/Production: Gene Cowan

The authors wish to acknowledge Annette Norwood for her assistance with research and proofreading.

Library of Congress Control Number: 2003107727
ISBN 0-87986-095-2

Copyright © 2003 National Council for the Social Studies
All rights reserved. No part of this publication may be reproduced, stored in a retrieval system, or transmitted, in any form or by any means, electronic, mechanical, photocopying, recording, or otherwise, without the prior written permission of the copyright holder.

Printed in the United States of America
5 4 3 2 1

# Contents

curr
300.71
p29

# PART TWO: TEACHING THE SOCIAL STUDIES: CHALLENGES AND PROSPECTS

# Introduction

"I've got a new student from Guatemala who speaks no English—how can I make her feel more included and welcomed in my classroom?"

"Apparently one of my students from Vietnam was an 'A' student in his home country. But he's only been in the U.S. for a year—what can I expect from him now?"

"How can I help my ELL students understand complex social studies concepts when their English isn't strong?"

"I hear my ELL students speaking to their friends in English; why can't they do the work in my class?"

"Should I advise parents to speak to their children in their native language at home—or is it better for them to try to speak English at home?"

"How do I assess ELL students' progress in my social studies classroom?"

"... but I'm a social studies teacher—I'm not trained in ESOL. Help!"

As teacher educators, we have been asked these questions time and again by current and prospective teachers. We've become acutely aware of the fact that most regular classroom teachers do not receive specialized training or preparation in teaching English Language Learners (ELLs). Although 42 percent of public school teachers have at least one ELL student in their classrooms, only 30 percent of these teachers have received training.[1]

Yet, the number of ELL students in our nation's classrooms continues to grow. According to the annual survey conducted by the U.S. Department of Education's Office of English Language Acquisition (OELA),[2] nearly 10 percent of the total public school enrollment of pre-K through 12th grade students has limited proficiency in English.[3]

While the immigration of families with children to the United States is certainly not new, what has changed is *how* those children are educated. At the turn of the twentieth century, the goal of education was to "Americanize" immigrant children and in many cases erase all vestiges of their native cultures, including their home languages. The school's primary mission was to create loyal citizens, well-versed in the nation's laws, conventions, and language.

But by the latter part of the twentieth century, educators began to question the educational soundness and equity of merely "Americanizing" students. The Civil Rights Movement heralded a major paradigm shift—one that shifted the blame of school failure from the students to that of their system of schooling.[4] It was clear that although some students were getting by academically in the "sink or swim" method of

English learning, many more were dropping out of schooling that did not meet their special cultural and linguistic needs. This is particularly tragic given that the workplace increasingly demands literacy and that many employers require a high school diploma or a higher level of education.

Today, the United States continues to be enriched by immigrants from countries the world over. Many cities have ethnic enclaves of language minority and immigrant groups, and these populations are reflected in school classrooms. Hispanics are in the process of becoming the largest ethnic minority group in the United States. For many of these children, Spanish is the first language learned and continues to be the main language spoken in the home. As such, Spanish-speaking children make up the bulk of our ELL students, although the nation's classrooms are populated by students from every country on the globe.

For decades California, Texas, and New York have integrated the majority of the country's immigrants into their communities and schools. Now, newcomers from other nations have begun settling throughout the United States, in every type of setting: rural, urban, suburban and beyond. Educating language minority students is no longer an issue only for states that have traditionally received a large number of immigrants. Schools in places like Lincoln, Nebraska now provide special assistance to ELL students. Alabama, another state that until recently has not had many ELL students, has seen its ELL population increase over 400 percent, and Idaho has had a 250 percent increase in the number of ELL students needing services in the state during the 1990s.[5]

According to the United States Census 2000 Supplementary Survey, in approximately 18 percent of U.S. households a language other than English is spoken. Between 1990 and 2000, the number of children aged 5 to 17 in English-speaking families increased 11 percent. In contrast, during the same decade there was a startling 55 percent increase in children of the same age living in households where languages other than English are spoken.[6] These population trends have had a marked effect on schools throughout the United States. Data from 1995 show that over 40 percent of teachers in the United States have one or more English Language Learners in their class.[7] In fact, between 1990 and 2001, the ELL population in the U.S. grew over 100 percent to more than 4 million students.[8] This trend continues to increase, and it has become clear that most educators must become skilled in teaching ELL students.

This book was written in response to the growing need for all teachers, and in particular social studies teachers, to provide comprehensible and appropriate instruction for students learning English. These students' degrees of English proficiency can vary from no comprehension whatsoever to strong conversational skills but weak academic language use. This means that a social studies teacher at any grade level can have an ELL student who knows absolutely no English but is expected to participate in instruction, as well as another ELL student who can speak English well but cannot comprehend academic texts. As is the case with teaching multilevel classes and adapting instruction for special needs, reaching each ELL student requires knowledgeable and skilled teachers who are keenly attuned to their students' needs, plan varied and flexible lessons, and follow through with extra support and assistance as needed.

## Which Students Get Classified as English Language Learners?

English Language Learners are often classified as Limited English Proficient (LEP) and placed in Bilingual Education or English as a Second Language (ESL) classes, if these are available. In traditional ESL approaches, as ELL students' comprehension and facility in English increases, they are first mainstreamed into elective courses with a high hands-on component, such as art, music, and physical education. Then, under the erroneous assumption that computation is less language dependent, ELL students are then placed into math and/or science classes.[9] Placement into regular social studies classes, with their emphasis on abstract concepts and

higher-order questions typically comes later. Of course, if the school district or school does not offer specialized language support, ELL students may be placed in content courses right away. This faster approach to mainstreaming has become a growing national trend. Because of that trend, one of the major aims of this book is to help teachers who have ELL students who were mainstreamed into social studies classes from their first day at school.

While students often master conversational English in two to three years, it can take much longer to develop academic use of a language.[10] Virginia Collier maintains that it takes a *minimum* of four years for non-native speakers of English to attain sufficient proficiency for school work.[11]

Jim Cummins has written extensively about the dilemma of ELL students. On the one hand, these students are learning English as a second (or third or fourth) language while simultaneously being acculturated into a new culture and society. On the other, they also need to continue their development of academic skills and the acquisition of content knowledge.

What is the best approach in supporting the development of English language skills while also progressing in content courses? Jo Ann Crandall reports that content-centered language learning is not only possible, but is crucial for the overall educational development of the student.[12] She reports that instructional strategies such as cooperative learning, task-based or experiential learning, whole language approach, and graphic organizers are central to a cognitive academic learning approach.

Today, these efforts have resulted in placing newly arrived students in classes based on age rather than English ability. This means that students must acquire language ability and social studies content knowledge simultaneously, and are often held accountable on proficiency tests in history or government.[13] As ELL students' English proficiency increases, they are able to comprehend more complex concepts in social studies, yet during this process a gap in knowledge of the subject between them and their English speaking peers must be closed. The ELL students have a double task of learning a language and content. If teachers are uninformed about facilitating both processes simultaneously, the gap will further widen.

For the social studies teacher, having ELL students in class can provide a number of challenges since the content area is so closely linked with literacy and language skills. The language of the social sciences is often abstract and includes complex concepts calling for higher-order skills. It can be a challenge to tailor lessons to meet the special needs of students who are English Language Learners. Additionally, social studies classes do not tend to be well-equipped with manipulatives and hands-on instructional materials, unlike other content areas such as math and science.[14]

But along with the challenges, there are a number of attendant positives. Immigrant children can offer alternate perspectives on historical events and political debates, shed light on cultural practices and governmental policies, and contribute cultural artifacts that can illuminate geographic studies. Social studies classes also have natural benefits and connections for ELL students: the inclusion of culture, the clarification of American traditions and mores, and the explanation of U.S. governmental practices, just to name a few.

## Why This Book?

This publication was driven by the desperate need for a book for social studies educators on teaching the English Language Learner. Although several excellent general books exist on teaching English to speakers of other languages (TESOL), there are none that specifically focus on the issues and content particular to the social studies.

There are three distinct sections in this book. The first section, "Getting to Know the ELL Student," is organized by K-12 social studies teachers' most commonly asked questions. These questions have been culled from our students, from teachers in the field, and from our own personal experiences. While teaching social studies content and skills provides some unique challenges, the social studies curriculum also presents teachers with ample opportunities for contextualized teaching, hands-on learning, and helping ELL students to learn more about the history and society of their new home while sharing experiences and perspectives from their home cultures.

In the second section, "Teaching the Social Studies: Challenges and Prospects," specific issues are discussed and examples of strategies and learning activities are provided. The lessons and activities were developed with the latest research findings in mind—as well as our own experiences and those of practicing teachers. Many of the lessons are "discourse rich," that is, giving students the opportunity to engage in high-level thought and engaging discussion that has been found to be particularly effective in second language learning.[15] Many educators have reported the efficacy of collaborative verbal interaction wherein ELL students can be encouraged to engage in discussion "without concern about their accents or possible grammatical errors."[16] Teachers will find that the approaches used are also effective for students with weak English language skills, even if they are not from homes in which a foreign language is spoken.

Finally, the third section directs teachers to additional resources, websites, and professional organizations. A Glossary at the end also provides useful definitions of terms used in the book and in the field. Interspersed throughout the text will be "Teachers' Stories," accounts of the actual experiences of social studies teachers' with ELL students.

## How to Use This Book

We recommend reading Part I in its entirety first. It will help contextualize and explain the central issues and controversies in English Language Learning. It will also provide the common language and terms later used in some of the learning activities and lessons in Part II. An introduction to the field will help the reader modify existing social studies lessons and materials.

Part II is divided into the five principal content areas taught by most social studies teachers: United States History, World History, Geography, Government and Civics, and Economics. We recommend that you first read those chapters most pertinent to your teaching for immediate ideas and strategies. However, you should also peruse the other subject areas, as they will likely provide other techniques and approaches that can be utilized and adapted to your classroom needs.

Because the lessons in this book focus on the effective teaching of social studies content through the use of appropriate methods for developing English proficiency in students (e.g., comprehensible instruction, communicative interaction), they address the three standards for Goal 2 of the *ESL Standards for Pre-K–12 Students* published by the educational association Teachers of English to Speakers of Other Languages.[17] They are as follows:

Goal 2—To use English to achieve academically in all content areas.

   Standard 1—Students will use English to interact in the classroom.

   Standard 2—Students will use English to obtain, process, construct, and provide subject matter information in spoken and written form.

   Standard 3—Students will use appropriate learning strategies to construct and apply academic knowledge.

We hope that the reader will find many practical, teacher-friendly strategies and techniques that have been shown to be effective not only with ELL students, but *all* students.

## Notes

1. Mei Han and David Baker, *A Profile of Policies and Practices for Limited English Proficient Students* (Washington, D.C.: Office of Educational Research and Improvement, 1997).

2. The Office of English Language Acquisition (OELA) was formerly known as the Office for Bilingual Education and Minority Languages Affairs (OBEMLA).

3. Anneka Kindler, *Survey of the States' Limited English Proficient Students and Available Educational Programs and Services* (Washington, D.C.: National Clearinghouse for English Language Acquisition and Language Instruction Educational Programs, 2002).

4. Deborah Menkart, *Multicultural Education: Strategies for Linguistically Diverse Schools and Classrooms.* National Council for Bilingual Education Program Information Guide Series, No. 16, 1993. Retrieved August 23, 2002 from http://www.ncbe.gwu.edu/ncbepubs/pigs/pig16.htm.

5. National Council for Bilingual Education, 1999. Retrieved September 24, 2002 from http://www.ncela.gwu.edu.

6. United States Census 2000 Supplementary Survey (Washington, D.C.: U.S. Bureau of the Census, 2002). Retrieved September 24, 2002 from http://www.census.gov/main/www/cen2000.html.

7. Marc Moss and Michael Puma, *Prospects: The Congressionally Mandated Study of Educational Opportunity and Growth: Language Minority and Limited English Proficiency Students* (Washington, D.C.: U.S. Department of Education, 1995).

8. Anneka L. Kindler, *op. cit.*: 3.

9. Deborah J. Short, *The Challenge of Social Studies for Limited English Proficient Students* (Washington, D.C.: Center for Applied Linguistics, 1993).

10. Jim Cummins, *BICS and CALP: Clarifying the Distinction* (ERIC Document Reproduction Service No. ED 438 551, 1999).

11. Virginia P. Collier, "The Effect of Age on Acquisition of a Second Language for School," *Forum*, no. 2 (Winter 1998) (ERIC Document Reproduction Service No. ED 296 580).

12. JoAnn Crandall, *Content-Centered Language Learning* (Washington, D.C.: ERIC Clearinghouse on Languages and Linguistics. ERIC Document Reproduction Service No. ED 367 142, 1994).

13. Denise McKeon, "When Meeting 'Common' Standards is Uncommonly Difficult," *Educational Leadership* 51, no. 8 (May 1994): 45-50; Kathleen Anderson Steeves, *Working Together to Strengthen History Teaching in Secondary Schools.* The American Historical Association (n.d.), Retrieved June 21, 2002 from http://www.theaha.org/pubs/Steeves.html# 14

14. Short, 1993.

15. Office of Educational Research and Improvement (OERI), *Integrating Language and Content: Lessons from Immersion* (Washington, D.C.: ERIC Clearinghouse on Languages and Linguistics, 1995).

16. Joy Egbert and Carmen Simich-Dudgeon, "Providing Support for Non-Native Learners of English in the Social Studies Classroom," *The Social Studies* 92, no. 1 (2001): 23.

17. Teachers of English to Speakers of Other Languages (TESOL), *ESL Standards for Pre-K–12 Students* (Alexandria, VA: TESOL, 1997).

## Other Useful Resources

August, Diane and Kenji Hakuta. *Language-Minority Children.* Washington, D.C.: National Academy Press, 1998. Retrieved August 23, 2002 from http://books.nap.edu/books/0309064147/html/index.html.

Chamot, Anna U. and J. M. O'Malley. *The CALLA Handbook: How to Implement the Cognitive Academic Language Learning Approach.* Reading, MA: Addison Wesley, 1994.

Flaitz, Jeffra (ed.). *Understanding Your International Students: A Cultural, Education, and Linguistic Guide.* Ann Arbor, MI: University of Michigan Press, 2003.

Ovando, Carlos J., Virginia P. Collier, and Mary Carol Combs. *Bilingual and ESL Classrooms.* Boston: McGraw Hill, 2003.

# Part 1

# Getting to Know the ELL Student

# CHAPTER 1

# Getting to Know the ELL Student: What Can I Expect?

## Does every social studies teacher need to know how to teach English language learners?

"I've been happy in Nebraska, but until recently I thought I had to choose between loving a particular rural place and experiencing all the beautiful diversity of the world .... However, in the last fifteen years something surprising has happened .... Now we [Lincoln, Nebraska] are one of the top-twenty cities in America for new arrivals from abroad. Our nonwhite population has grown 128 percent since 1990 .... We have children from fifty different nationalities who speak thirty-two different languages in our public schools."[1]

As Mary Pipher notes above, linguistic diversity has now reached even the most unlikely resettlement communities, and their schools are enrolling immigrants and refugees from around the world. In every part of the United States, English Language Learners (ELL) are an increasing presence in our schools, and all teachers need to know how to help them reach high levels of academic achievement. Social studies teachers in particular play a very crucial role in educating ELL students since most program models mainstream these students into social studies classes from the moment they enroll in school. Although many ELL students may initially take their language arts classes in a sheltered, or language-supported, environment with other ELL students and a trained English for Speakers of Other Languages (ESOL) specialist, most ELL students are assigned to regular social studies classes whether they can understand a word of English or not. Although making instruction comprehensible to these students may seem like an impossible task, there are a number of strategies and techniques that excellent social studies teachers use to reach ELL students at various stages of language proficiency.

## Who is the ELL student?

Melissa teaches social studies to 9th graders in Florida. Her city is a retirement mecca for Midwesterners who moved south to avoid the cold. Until a few years ago, most of the kids in her school were children of local residents who worked in the hotel and health care fields. With each passing year, her students' backgrounds began to change. The first English language learner whom Melissa taught was from Laos, the child of a former political prisoner who was resettled in the area by the federal government. Not only did Melissa have to learn how to teach social studies to Khampane, she also had to learn how to communicate with her student's parents, who were recovering physically and emotionally from the torture and deprivation experienced in prison camps. Not long after beginning to teach Khampane, Melissa welcomed two Mexican students, Felipe and Manuel, whose families shifted from migrant work to housekeeping in nearby hotels. Felipe and Manuel had never attended school previously, and the speed with which they acquired English was seriously hindered by their lack of literacy in Spanish. She often paired one of them up with another Spanish-speaking ELL student named Raúl, a well-educated, affluent student from Venezuela whose father was transferred into management at a local biotechnology company. Raúl knew no English when he arrived, but his rate of progress was very rapid, and Melissa thought that some of his talent might rub off on the other Spanish speakers. Most recently, Melissa's class made room for Adisa, a student from Bosnia. Adisa had done very well in school in Bosnia, but her education had been interrupted by war, and she held a deep resentment for having to leave her homeland. Because of Adisa's educational background, Melissa expected her to catch on quickly, but Adisa's resentment turned into hostility that Melissa was unable to lessen. Many of the local students infuriated Adisa because they had no understanding of, or sympathy for, her experience living through war, and when she tried to explain her experience to them, they made fun of her accent.

Overwhelmed by the degree of cultural and linguistic diversity in her classroom, Melissa began asking her colleagues for help in meeting the disparate learning needs of her students. "How can I be expected to teach students who are native speakers of English in the same class with students who are learning English? What are the cultural and linguistic differences that I need to know about in order to teach these students effectively? Can somebody help me, please?!"

Educators are expected to teach increasingly diverse classes, and the diversity that exists between the various cultures and languages of ELL students can be even greater than the differences between ELL students and their native-speaker classmates. English language learners come from various educational, linguistic, socioeconomic, and cultural backgrounds, and they are also at different points on the English language acquisition continuum, on which progress is also affected by students' different learning abilities, rates, and styles. There is no monolithic ELL student for whom a teacher can plan. Each teacher must become familiar with the background and level of English proficiency of every ELL student in order to plan appropriate lessons and modifications to instruction. Nonetheless, knowing some basic information about the languages and cultures of ELL students can help teachers relate to and understand their needs. The following table lists the ten primary languages of origin of English language learners in the United States.

| Language | Percentage of U.S. ELL Students |
|---|---|
| Spanish | 76.6 |
| Vietnamese | 2.3 |
| Hmong | 2.2 |
| Haitian Creole | 1.1 |
| Korean | 1.1 |
| Cantonese | 1.0 |
| Arabic | 0.9 |
| Russian | 0.9 |
| Navajo | 0.9 |
| Tagalog | 0.8 |
| Cambodian | 0.7 |

Source: Survey of States' LEP Students and Available Educational Programs and Services 1999-2000 Summary Report, The National Clearinghouse for English Language Acquisition. (2001). http://www.ncbe.gwu.edu/ncbepubs/seareports/99-00/sea9900.pdf retrieved September 1, 2002.

Although Spanish is by far the most common first language of English language learners in the U.S., this can vary according to the area of the country. Moreover, Spanish-speaking ELL students come from diverse countries and cultures with, for example, many students from Caribbean countries in Florida and New York and from Mexico and Central America in Texas and California. Even though most English language learners in the U.S. speak Spanish as their first language, most American schools enroll ELL students from many different first languages and cultures. Despite this range of diversity, when considering English language learners in general, there are common principles of second language acquisition and teaching that apply to various situations. As you read through the book, you will learn numerous teaching strategies that apply to ELL students from a variety of backgrounds.

**What are some popular acronyms used in the field?**
Every field has its own jargon, but this field has an especially tricky list of acronyms that confound even the well-informed. A primary difficulty is the variety of accepted designations for students who are learning English, which are listed below under "Terms for the Students." Some of the most common acronyms are:

Terms for the Students
- English Language Learner (ELL): Currently the most popular term in the literature, this term is used to describe non-native speakers who are learning English.
- Limited English Proficient (LEP) student: A federal term that is used in reports, grant guidelines and many official documents. This term has lost favor in the field, as it denotes limitations rather than potential. Certain states have renamed the acronym LEP to Language Enriched Pupil, emphasizing the benefits of bilingualism.
- Potential English Proficient (PEP) student: Sometimes used as an alternative to LEP in federal documents.

Terms for the Subject or Program Area
- English for Speakers of Other Languages (ESOL): Describes the subject of English for Speakers of Other Languages; for example, non-native speakers who study English are ESOL students, just as pupils who study social studies are social studies students. The acronym ESOL is used primarily in pre-K–12 and adult education settings.

- English as a Second Language (ESL): Used primarily in post-secondary settings, such as university intensive English programs for international students. ESL is a subject area, just like ESOL, and sometimes the terms are used interchangeably.
- English as a Foreign Language (EFL): Refers to teaching English in countries/locations where it is not the first language of the majority of the population. This is analogous to the teaching of foreign languages in the U.S. (e.g., German), and it is a subject matter like ESL and ESOL.
- English as a New Language (ENL): Used as an alternative to ESOL and ESL.
- English as an Additional Language (EAL): Less common term for ESOL and ESL.
- Bilingual Education: This is an approach to teaching English to non-native speakers that supports the learning of content in their native languages; this reduces the achievement gap that occurs while ELL students are learning English and thereby do not possess the language skills to comprehend complex topics taught in the majority language until they are sufficiently proficient in English. There are a variety of models of bilingual education, from transitional approaches that move students into increasing use of English for various subject areas, to dual language or two-way programs, whose goal is to provide instruction in two languages for English language learners as well as their native English-speaking schoolmates. Dual language programs typically use a structured, supported, sheltered immersion approach to teach content in Spanish to English-speaking students, and English to Spanish-speaking students, with some subjects taught in the native languages as well.

Terms for Specializations within the Subject Area
- English for Academic Purposes (EAP): English study that focuses solely on developing academic language rather than a broader focus that includes conversational skills, cultural skills, and so forth.
- English for Specific Purposes (ESP): English study that focuses on the specialized vocabulary of a particular trade or subject area. For example, the study of English for business or for medicine/ health care would be in ESP classes.

Terms for the Professional Organizations
- Teachers of English to Speakers of Other Languages (TESOL): The professional organization of the ESOL teaching field.
- American Council on the Teaching of Foreign Languages (ACTFL): The professional organization of the foreign language teaching field.
- National Association for Bilingual Education (NABE): The professional organization that promotes English language development through bilingual education and heritage language maintenance.

Technical Terms
- Second Language Acquisition (SLA): The process of learning a second (or third, etc.) language, this term also is the name for the scholarly field of inquiry that informs ESOL instructional practice.
- First Language (L1), Second Language (L2): Terms used to denote students' first and second languages. C1 and C2 are also used to denote students' first and second cultures.

## By law, what kind of education am I required to provide to ESOL students in my social studies classroom?

Federal law is very specific regarding the rights of ELL students. In 1974, the landmark case *Lau vs. Nichols* was argued before the U.S. Supreme Court. The ruling stated that regardless of students' English proficiency, they are entitled to "a meaningful opportunity to participate in the public educational program." According to the ruling, this can be accomplished through teaching ESOL or bilingual education to ELL students. The ruling affirmed: "There is no equality of treatment merely by providing students with the same facilities, textbooks, teachers, and curriculum; for students who do not understand English are effectively foreclosed from any meaningful education." (*Lau v. Nichols*, 1974).

Different states have chosen different approaches, with some emphasizing bilingual education and others ESOL. Bilingual education models include varying proportions of native language instruction, which decrease as the students become more proficient in English. Most ESOL programs involve a three-pronged approach: (a) Mainstreamed content instruction, taught by ESOL-trained content area teachers who use ESOL approaches to promote comprehension and achievement; (b) Sheltered (ELL students only) ESOL instruction focusing on language development, taught by educators with specialized ESOL credentials; and (c) Bilingual support, when feasible, provided by a paraprofessional or other interpreter.

Your role as a social studies teacher pertains to the first category above, and as a content area teacher, you are the most important contributor to your ELL students' success. You play this key role because ELL students spend far more time in mainstream classes than in sheltered classes and because social studies requires more language use, both verbal and written, than most other content areas (e.g., mathematics). You can make instruction comprehensible to ELL students at various levels of English proficiency by using ESOL approaches described in this book, such as modified input and interaction in your teaching (see p. 23 below), as well as through developing an effective partnership with ESOL specialists and bilingual aides. By law, you are charged with providing equitable, comprehensible instruction for ELL students in your class. As a knowledgeable and informed educator, you will find that adapting your teaching to the needs of ELL students will become a natural part of your planning and instruction.

### Why should I know something about schooling in my ELL students' native countries?

Students' prior educational experiences affect their expectations about and performance in school in the U.S. Depending on students' age of arrival in the U.S., their experience in schools in their native countries or lack thereof, and their native culture's perspective on education and schooling, ELL students will vary in their adjustment to the prevailing educational practices and procedures in the U.S. Even if a child never attended school in the native country, her or his parents have culturally-based opinions on the importance of school and attitudes about sound approaches to teaching and learning. For example, in some immigrant cultures, sharing work and helping classmates is considered an important part of learning; yet when students from these cultures share their answers with classmates during tests, teachers in the U.S. often view this as cheating and punish the students without asking whether they understood that such behavior was not appropriate in schools here. In certain Asian cultures, the primary means of learning is through rote memorization, so when some Asian students are put in cooperative groups to solve a problem, they may view this as non-academic and a waste of time. The following table describes the predominant

educational models used in ELL countries of origin.

While the generalizations noted above can be helpful, it is also important to remember that each student is a unique individual and may not identify with the prevailing conditions of his or her home country.

### How might ELL students' background knowledge and prior schooling impact instruction in a social studies classroom?

English language learners bring rich experiences and knowledge to the classroom, and their lack of English proficiency does not equal lack of intelligence or potential. If you are teaching children who have been schooled in their countries of origin, it is possible that you will teach them information and concepts that they already know in their native language.

Background knowledge gained from prior experience and schooling is a distinct advantage in mastering the content as well as in learning the related English vocabulary. Imagine having to learn about the French Revolution in Vietnamese without ever having studied this historical event versus knowing the main facts and events in English first and then assigning Vietnamese terms to them. In the first case, you might not get more than the basic gist of the topic, even if the teacher used visuals such as maps, pictures, and graphs. In the second case, since you know the topic, you would know the big picture, and it would be easier to learn the details in a second language.

One theory states that, in order to comprehend text (oral or written), we must draw from information stored in our brains in clusters called schemata.[3] These schemata help us assign meaning to words and phrases. Each individual has had different experiences, and schemata reflect this. For example, if a child has watched or played baseball, then a book about a visit to the ballpark will make more sense. Much of what children read assumes that they share a certain cultural background, and English language learners often miss key pieces of information due to cultural differences. A math problem showing a picture of a little girl blowing out eight candles on a cake followed by the question, "How old is the girl?" requires cultural knowledge that many ELL students may not have. For tips on how to help ELL students develop the schema necessary to comprehend lesson content, please see Chapter 3, below, pp. 25-26.

The researcher Jim Cummins has found that students who have developed reading and writing skills in their

| Country | Teaching Styles | Learning Styles | Exams |
|---|---|---|---|
| Colombia | Teacher-centered with note-taking, lectures, and dictation. | Many students are kinesthetic and visual, but students are expected to stay still and listen. | Dictation, fill-in-the-blanks, true/false, and multiple choice |
| Cuba | Teacher-centered with lectures. | Lots of individual work, with memorization and homework. | Midterms and finals |
| Haiti | Teacher-fronted lectures. Teachers do not help students analyze and synthesize. Corporal punishment is allowed in school and at home. | Rote learning and memorization. Students speak only when called upon. Grades are more important than learning. | National exams in the 3rd, 6th, and 9th grades |
| Korea | Teacher is the giver of knowledge and lectures in front of class—discussion is rare. There is a lot of homework. | Rote memorization. Students ask few questions for fear of shame for not understanding. | 1 hour essay exams in each subject |
| Mexico | Teacher-fronted, with students listening, but educational reform is now emphasizing more active learning. | There is a preference for memorization since the tests emphasize facts and figures. Students prefer lots of structure. Many students prefer a global approach to learning. Students are used to working alone and in groups. Kinesthetic activities are well received. | Multiple-choice, open-ended, and true/false subject midterms and finals |
| Vietnam | Teacher-fronted lectures. Students can be singled out for questioning. Dictations and note-taking are common. Memorization of long passages is emphasized. Some reform has taken hold, with an interest in more innovative pedagogical techniques. | Students work individually and rarely ask questions in class. The student is responsible for understanding the material. Homework is very important. Parents are very involved in school. | Dictations, recitations, daily oral quizzes, and midterms and finals |

native language are able to progress much more rapidly in developing English literacy than those who have no literacy skills in any language.[4] Moreover, he found that students who have acquired academic language, or what he terms Cognitive Academic Language Proficiency (CALP), in their native language are able to acquire academic language in English faster and more efficiently. This means that an ELL who had no schooling or interrupted schooling in the native country will take longer to develop academic language proficiency in English than one who was better educated.

One additional issue related to a student's background knowledge is the nature of the native language. Certain language systems, such as French or German, are closer in nature to English than others, such as Chinese or Vietnamese. Being bilingual provides many cognitive advantages regardless of the first language (please see Chapter 2, below, p. 20), but the structure of the native language will affect how quickly the student (especially older children) will acquire oral and literacy skills in English.

When planning lessons, social studies teachers need to ask themselves about any prior knowledge that is required to comprehend the topic and build in activities that contextualize the topic and the requisite background knowledge. Please see Chapter 3, pp. 25-26 for guidance on using prior knowledge and contextualization.

### Notes

1. Mary Pipher, *The Middle of Everywhere: The World's Refugees Come to Our Town* (New York: Harcourt, 2002): 5-6.

2. Adapted from Jeffra Flaitz (ed.), *Understanding Your International Students: A Cultural, Educational, and Linguistic Guide* (Ann Arbor, MI: University of Michigan Press, 2003).

3. Patricia L. Carrell, and Joan C. Eisterhold, "Schema Theory and ESL Reading Pedagogy," in Michael H. Long and Jack C. Richards (eds.), *Methodology in TESOL: A Book of Readings* (New York: Newbury House, 1987): 218-232.

4. Jim Cummins, "The Role of Primary Language Development in Promoting Educational Success for Language Minority Students," in *Schooling and Language Minority Students: A Theoretical Framework* (California State Department of Education, 1981), 3-49.

# CHAPTER 2

# Getting to Know the ELL Student: Focus on Language

## Introduction

We believe that the best preparation for any teacher of an English language learner places primary focus on language and communication. Through understanding the second language acquisition process, effective communication strategies, and measures that enhance language development, the social studies teacher can go beyond simple teaching strategies to meet the needs of ELL children. The following questions pertain to language issues and are the foundation upon which effective teaching of ELL students is built.

Although you may think of yourself as a social studies teacher, when you have one or more ELL students in your class, you become a language teacher, too. There is an approach to teaching subject matter to ELL students called content-based instruction, which considers teachers' goals as follows:

1. To provide comprehensible instruction, ensuring that ELL students understand the content of the lesson—through modified communication and teaching/assessment strategies, including native language support; and
2. To promote English language development—through providing comprehensible instruction that enables ELL students to connect the meaning and form of language, as well as by providing numerous opportunities for meaningful language use in interaction with peers who are more proficient in English and/or with the teacher.

This chapter discusses elements of the content-based instruction approach and other strategies for helping ELL students comprehend social studies lessons while developing their English proficiency.

## What can I expect ELL students to do in my class?

Becoming proficient in English, and even more so in academic English, is a long process. Learners go through a fairly regular sequence, regardless of their native languages. For learners from certain first language backgrounds, there may be substages within the sequence, and some learners may progress at slower or faster rates based on a variety of factors, including native language, age, affective issues, and so on.

A good first step in understanding how to help ELL students learn social studies is becoming familiar with the stages of second language acquisition (SLA). There are many models of the process of SLA, but one simple model based on the teaching approach, called the Natural Approach, has been very useful to content area teachers who work with ELL students.[1] It is important to note that this model varies according to learner characteristics and that the stages are fluid and not discrete.

The Natural Approach segments the complex process of SLA into four basic levels and details student and teacher behaviors at each one. Knowing the characteristics of each level equips teachers to communicate effectively with ELL students and to select appropriate teaching strategies. A brief description of each level follows, including a reproducible master of an abbreviated matrix of the levels for categorizing your ELL students accordingly. The learning activities that are included in the social studies chapters later in this book are organized and categorized using these four levels.

### Level 1—Preproduction

Students at the preproduction stage have anywhere from ten hours to six months of exposure to English and are just beginning to learn the language. In class they may be shy and will mainly listen and respond non-verbally. Many teachers mistakenly push these students to speak English before they are ready. For most ELL students at this level, it is very important for them to have time to listen and absorb the language before they are required to speak it. This is sometimes referred to as the "Silent Period." As they move through this level, their vocabulary includes approximately 500 receptive words (words they can understand but don't use yet), and they are beginning to develop Basic Interpersonal Communication Skills (BICS), which is language used for social communication. At this level, the teacher should be doing about 90 percent or more of the talking, and the ELL students should listen and respond non-verbally. In order for the teacher's speech to be comprehensible, it should include lots of pantomime, body language, facial expressions, and gestures. In addition, the teacher should *model*—rather than just verbally explain—tasks and skills, and use lots of pictures and real objects whenever possible. The teacher's speech should be simplified, slow, and clear. ELL students at this level can be involved in lessons if the teacher checks their comprehension by asking them to respond non-verbally. For example, they can point to an item, nod to answer simple yes/no questions, and carry out simple commands (e.g., put the globe on the table).

## Level 2—Early Production

At this level, students have had anywhere from three months to a year of exposure to English. They can now begin to produce some language, in the form of one- to two-word responses along with the same type of non-verbal responses that they depended on in Level 1. About 1,000 words form their receptive vocabulary, and, as at any other level, about 10 percent of their vocabulary is expressive (words they regularly use). The types of questions that students can answer at this level are yes/no, "what" questions that elicit one- to two-word responses (what is this?), "who" questions (who is standing next to the equator on the floor map?), "either/or questions" (is this an ocean or a sea?) and "where" questions that require a simple phrase response (where is the Matterhorn?—In Switzerland). Formulaic chunks of language are emerging as well, with most of the elements of the chunks remaining unanalyzed. For example, they may be able to use the phrase, "How ya doin'?" but they may not be able to understand the function of each word and how the words should form a sentence.

Teachers must be careful to ask students questions that are appropriate for their level and to use simplified language, avoiding idioms, colloquial expressions, and uncommon vocabulary. Using the master on page 18 to categorize students into appropriate levels will help you to remember which questions and strategies you should use for each ELL student in your class.

Because students develop expressive skills in English at the early production stage, they can communicate in a simple manner with their classmates in pairs and small groups. Interacting with peers to solve problems, develop projects, discuss class topics, etc., provides better opportunities for ELL students to understand the content as well as develop their language than many whole-class, teacher-directed activities. In whole-class activities, ELL students are usually reluctant to ask questions if they don't understand the lesson, but in a pair or small group activity, they may be less intimidated and ask for help. Also, in small group and pair activities, ELL students have greater opportunities to practice speaking (each person can speak, versus having the teacher ask the class a question, in which case only one person responds), and both partners can negotiate meaning, which means that if the native speaker doesn't understand the ELL student, she or he can ask for clarification or verification, and vice versa. Negotiation of meaning cannot be achieved unless ELL students can participate in conversation. Research has shown that the focus on accurately conveying meaning through two-way negotiation is a crucial condition for language development.

Once students have developed rudimentary vocabulary and syntax in English, they often progress rapidly. This limited vocabulary and syntax forms the basis on which they build their proficiency. By understanding and using a few words and phrases, ELL students can increase their receptive and expressive abilities in English more independently.

## Level 3—Speech Emergence

At this point, after somewhere between one and three years of exposure to English, the proficiency of ELL students increases exponentially. They use phrases and sentences, and their receptive vocabulary grows to nearly 7,000 words. Questions they are now able to answer include "how" and "why," which require fairly complex responses. Because they can understand a great deal and can express themselves fairly effectively, albeit with grammatical simplicity and developmental errors, ELL students at the Speech Emergence stage can participate in a variety of learning activities. General student-centered practices such as scaffolding and expansion, poetry, songs, chants, prediction, comparing/contrasting, describing, cooperative learning, problem solving, and drawing charts and graphs, are appropriate for ELL students, but the classroom teacher must provide them with additional support. This includes:

1. Analyzing the degree of cognitive complexity and contextual support contained in passages in English (see Chapter 3 for an explanation) and increasing the context appropriately;

2. Monitoring her or his own oral and written communication, including (a) the use of complex language structures (e.g., subordinate and relative clauses, the passive voice); (b) the use of idioms (e.g., using the term "brush up on" rather than "review/practice"); (c) the use of unusual vocabulary (e.g., "wheedle" versus "convince"), (d) the rate of speech; (e) the degree of redundancy and paraphrasing, and (f) the frequency of comprehension checks to determine whether the ELL student is actually following and understanding; and

3. Increasing the number of non-verbal cues, such as showing short video snippets, and providing diagrams such as concept maps and other graphic organizers. At every stage, whenever communication breaks down, the teacher should employ the same strategies as those used in the beginning stages, such as showing a picture, consulting a bilingual dictionary, gesturing and acting out, etc.

### Level 4—Intermediate Fluency

A shift occurs at this level, after about three to four years of exposure to English, because ELL students begin to develop Cognitive Academic Language Proficiency (CALP) in English (see the next question for an explanation). Having mastered the knowledge and skills required for social language (Basic Interpersonal Communication Skills), ELL students have accumulated a receptive vocabulary of approximately 12,000 words. They have gone beyond speaking in phrases and simple sentences to being able to engage in extended discourse. They can answer complex questions that require them to synthesize and evaluate information because they possess adequate academic language proficiency to do so in English. This means that they can participate in essay writing, complex problem solving, researching and supporting their positions, and critiquing and analyzing literature. Although it may seem that they are able to perform the same activities as native speakers, they continue to need special support until their Cognitive Academic Language Proficiency in English is fully developed and they have closed any gaps in their understanding of the subject as a result of concepts and skills that were taught prior to their developing adequate proficiency. These limitations can accumulate and cause students to fall farther and farther behind. Care must be taken to provide sufficient contextual support, as well as to assess and build the background knowledge required for learning any new topic.

The assessment of ELL students at this and all levels

of proficiency must be planned carefully. If the ability to compare and contrast political systems is measured by a test question that requires a grammatically correct essay response, then the objective is not truly being assessed. In many cases, alternative assessments that allow ELL students at this level to demonstrate achievement of a learning objective through creating diagrams, bulleted lists, and other less language-dependent means can improve validity and fairness. The important point to remember is that students at Level 4 are still in the process of learning academic English, and when they experience difficulty or fail to achieve minimum levels of performance, they likely require language support. (See Table 1.)

### If my ELL students can speak to their friends in English, why do they have difficulty doing my class work?

According to Jim Cummins, there are two types of language use, Basic Interpersonal Communication Skills (BICS) and Cognitive Academic Language Proficiency (CALP).[3] Language that students use to interact with others for social purposes is described as Basic Interpersonal Communication Skills. For example, talking with friends about a party, speaking with teachers about a hall pass, and discussing sports with coaches are social language, or BICS. For many English language learners in K-12, BICS is developed through social interaction. On the other hand, Cognitive Academic Language Proficiency, or CALP, is specialized language that is used for academic purposes. This academic language is acquired at school and is necessary to succeed in academic subjects. For example, explaining how historical events led to particular outcomes, comparing and contrasting the topography of two countries, and evaluating economic systems all require a high degree of CALP.

Some English language learners may have developed CALP in their native languages if they have had adequate schooling in their native countries. These ELL students have an advantage in developing CALP in English since they are familiar with the purpose and use of academic language and can transfer some of the concepts once they develop the English vocabulary and structure. English language learners who have not acquired CALP in their native language, especially those who have not attended school or had interrupted schooling in their native country, need greater support in developing CALP in English so that they can comprehend academic subjects.

**Table 1**
# English Language Learner Matrix
Adapted from J. Bell.[2]

| Preproduction | Early Production | Speech Emergence | Intermediate Fluency |
|---|---|---|---|
| **Learner Behaviors**<br>Points to items<br>Follows commands<br>Listens primarily | **Learner Behaviors**<br>One to two word responses<br>Labels and matches items<br>Lists items | **Learner Behaviors**<br>Phrases and simple sentences<br>Compare/contrast items<br>Describes items | **Learner Behaviors**<br>Beginning CALP<br>Dialogue and discourse<br>Reading and writing academic texts |
| **Teaching Strategies**<br>Gestures and acting out<br>Repetition<br>Pictures and props<br>Simple yes/no questions | **Teaching Strategies**<br>Models tasks and language<br>Simple role plays<br>Either/or questions<br>Who and where questions | **Teaching Strategies**<br>Focus content on key concepts<br>Frequent comprehension checks<br>Expanded vocabulary<br>How and why questions | **Teaching Strategies**<br>Provide alternative assessment<br>Check for language bias<br>Check for cultural bias<br>Provide contextual support |
| | | | |
| | | | |
| | | | |
| | | | |
| | | | |

Add your ELL students' names in the appropriate columns and keep this matrix in your grade book for frequent reference.

# Length of Time Required to Achieve Age-Appropriate Levels of Conversational and Academic Proficiency

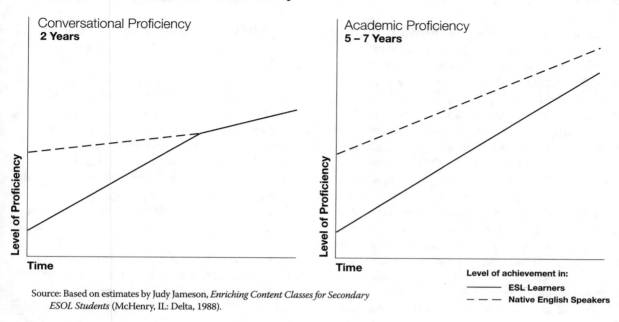

**Conversational Proficiency**
**2 Years**

Level of Proficiency

Time

**Academic Proficiency**
**5 – 7 Years**

Level of Proficiency

Time

Level of achievement in:
——— ESL Learners
– – – Native English Speakers

Source: Based on estimates by Judy Jameson, *Enriching Content Classes for Secondary ESOL Students* (McHenry, IL: Delta, 1988).

Since BICS is a simpler form of communication, developing it is a much quicker process than developing CALP. Jim Cummins estimates that it can take five to eight years for ELL students to develop sufficient CALP to achieve academic parity with native speakers of English. The above diagram indicates what often happens during the difficult task of expanding content knowledge, the learning of which is dependent upon communication ability in English, and developing English proficiency. The solid line depicts a hypothetical rate of expected progress in content knowledge for all students over a period of approximately eight years. The dashed line represents a hypothetical rate of second language development by ELL students, which must increase at a greater rate than that of content knowledge and skills in order for ELL students to catch up with their English-speaking peers. The point of well-planned mainstreaming programs for ELL students is to narrow and eventually close the gap.

## How can we help close the gap between ELL students' English language development and their level of achievement in the social studies?

In order to close the gap, educational programs must provide strong English language development support as well as comprehensible instruction in the various content areas. Content area instruction that is comprehensible to ELL students serves the double function of helping the students to master the content while providing a meaning-focused, context-rich environment that promotes language learning. If either of these components is inadequate, the gap will remain or even increase.

Even if English language learners can use social language with seeming perfection, their use of academic English may not be fully developed until years later. This gap will be apparent in their reading and writing of academic texts as well as in their achievement in the content areas. If the students have developed CALP in their native language, the gap can be closed sooner.

## Should ELL students spend their time studying English before they study social studies?

Although you are a social studies teacher, in many ways you are also an English teacher because you have an important role in assisting ELL students to expand their English proficiency. English language learners who are mainstreamed spend the majority, or often all, of the school day learning content in English, so this is the primary means of their developing English language competencies and skills. A way of teaching ELL students called the Cognitive Academic Language Learning Approach (CALLA), developed by Anna U. Chamot and J. Michael O'Malley, provides a structure to making subject matter content comprehensible to ELL students while developing their English proficiency.[4] This approach is a type of content-based second language instruction, which uses study of the subject area as a means for language development. If the focus is on providing comprehensible instruction and ensuring that communication and understanding have taken place, and if students have opportunities for interaction with peers that allows and supports negotiation of meaning, then there is compatibility in the goals of teaching content and developing English skills. Typically content-based instruction occurs in sheltered environments, where ELL students learn together and teachers pitch and pace their instruction to their students' level of proficiency. However, a similar outcome can be achieved if the ELL students are in a mainstream classroom where the principles of content-based instruction are followed to the degree that is feasible.

## How does learning a second language affect students' basic skills?

The question of basic skills is, of course, a critical one that always seems to be of concern to parents as well. It is often raised in the context of children learning a foreign language in elementary school, for example. Is learning another language going to be detrimental for my child? Will it impede her progress in reading or math? Fortunately, the answer in this respect is fairly straightforward. Children who learn another language to a certain level of proficiency perform as well as, or better than, monolingual children and are favorably prepared to be academically successful, as is suggested by a growing body of research that has found that:

- Knowing another language can lead to academic and cognitive benefits[5]
- The study of another language often correlates to higher scores on standardized measures of English, math, and social studies even for students from low socio-economic backgrounds[6]
- Operating in two languages can help children's metacognitive and metalinguistic development, cognitive flexibility, and divergent thinking[7]
- Bilingual students with a strong competency in two languages are more likely to be successful readers[8]
- The benefits from bilingualism are greater when children are *fluent* in both languages.[9] In other words, as Cummins suggested, a certain threshold level of proficiency in the second language is needed to achieve these benefits.[10] A child who is highly proficient in her second language will clearly benefit from positive cognitive consequences where the connection might not be as clear for a child with an average level of proficiency.[11]

## Should I advise parents to speak to their children in their native language at home, or is it better for them to try to speak English at home?

It seems as if the United States government invests millions of dollars annually teaching languages to adults who work in various sectors of the economy and to children in schools. Yet, very little effort is directed towards capitalizing on the assets that language minority children bring to our schools.[12] English language learners are often looked upon as a problem to be remedied rather than as a resource to the community. One could argue that maintaining the home languages of our students and supporting their development is a worthwhile challenge that will affect the ELL student's personal identity, academic success, cognitive development and ultimately benefit our society as a whole. As was pointed out above, a student with a high proficiency in both languages will derive much greater cognitive and academic benefits.

Research also cautions against withdrawing home language support too soon. The literature in the field points out that the support of home language reinforces the bond between the home and the school and facilitates communication at home between parents who might not be very proficient in English, and their children. In addition, if the children develop literacy skills in both languages, they may become functionally bilingual adults, leading to clear professional advantages.[13] Finally, communication between parents and children is critical, and asking parents to talk to their children in a language they may not speak well impedes communication.

## How can I communicate effectively with ELL students?

There are two important aspects of effective communication with ELL students: (1) modified input; and (2) modified interaction. Modified input includes everything that is directed specifically toward the ELL student(s). For example, teaching strategies that include providing pictures, speaking slowly and clearly, and focusing on the here and now are all forms of modified input. Modified input is an important but not sufficient factor in effective communication with ELL students. In addition, the type of interaction used between the teacher and ELL student, and the native speakers and ELL students in group activities, is an important element of effective communication. The interaction must be modified to scaffold the ELL student's comprehension and production of the language and content. For example, more frequent comprehension checks should be used as well as supported negotiation of meaning. This might include teaching ELL students phrases such as "please repeat that," "what does___ ___mean?" and "how do you say____?" and teaching other students in the group how to rephrase, expand, and check for indications of miscommunication. Paying attention to the student and teacher characteristics at each of the four proficiency levels will help you adjust your communication spontaneously. With practice, you will become fluent in modified input and interaction, and it will become second nature for you to gear both areas to individual students' needs. Teaching some of these skills to your native-speaking students will improve their abilities to communicate with others, and will help develop your ELL student's language skills more rapidly as well.

## Notes

1. Stephen D. Krashen and Tracy D. Terrell, *The Natural Approach: Language Acquisition in the Classroom* (Oxford: Pergamon, 1983).

2. Jill Bell, *Teaching Multilevel Classes in ESL* (Carlsbad, CA: Dominie Press, 1988).

3. James Cummins, *Bilingualism and Special Education: Issues in Assessment and Pedagogy* (San Diego: College-Hill, 1984).

4. Anna U. Chamot and J. Michael O'Malley, *The CALLA Handbook: Implementing the Cognitive Academic Language Learning Approach* (Reading, MA: Addison-Wesley, 1994).

5. Laurie Makin, Julie Campbell, and Criss Jones Diaz, *One Childhood, Many Languages* (Sydney: Harper Educational, 1995); M. Met, "Why Language Learning Matters," *Educational Leadership* 59, no. 2 (2001): 36-40.

6. Rudolph Masciantonio, "Tangible Benefits for the Study of Latin: A Review of Research," *Foreign Language Annals*, 10 (1977): 375-82; E. Rafferty, *Second Language Study and Basic Skills in Louisiana* (Baton Rouge: Louisiana Department of Education, 1986); S. J. Caldas and N. Bourdeaux, "Poverty, Race and Foreign Language Immersion: Predictors of Math and English Language Arts Performance," *Learning Languages* 5, no. 1 (1999): 4-15; D. W. Robinson, "The Cognitive, Academic, and Attitudinal Benefits of Early Language Learning," in M. Met (ed.), *Critical Issues in Early Language Learning* (Glenview, IL: Scott Foresman Addison-Wesley, 1998): 37-43.

7. Kenji Hakuta, *Mirror of Language: The Debate of Bilingualism* (New York: Basic, 1986); Robinson, *ibid.*

8. Kathryn Lindholm-Leary, *Biliteracy for a Global Society: An Idea Book on Dual Language Education* (Washington, D.C.: National Clearinghouse for Bilingual Education, 2000).

9. Connie Janssen and Anne Pauwels, *Raising Children Bilingually in Australia* (Clayton, Victoria: Language and Society Center, 1993).

10. James Cummins, "The Role of Primary Language Development in Promoting Educational Success for Language Minority Students," in *Schooling and Language Minority Students: A Theoretical Framework* (Los Angeles: Evaluation, Dissemination, and Assessment Center, California State University, 1981).

11. Fred Genesee, *Learning Through Two Languages: Studies of Immersion and Bilingual Education* (Rowley, MA: Newbury House, 1987).

12. Met, 2001.

13. ERIC Digest, "Myths and Misconceptions about Second Language Learning," ERIC Clearinghouse on Languages and Linguistics Washington DC. ED350885. (ERIC, 2000).

# CHAPTER 3

# Teaching ELL Students: Where Do I Begin?

## Introduction

The best place to begin is to understand the second language acquisition process and to consider effective communication as the primary goal in your classroom. If English language learners do not understand what you as the teacher, or their classmates are conveying, then acquiring the English language and learning the social studies content cannot occur. Stephen D. Krashen clearly distinguishes the terms "acquiring" and "learning."[1] "Acquiring" is a developmental process that occurs when the language, such as English, is presented in a natural, meaningful way. However, the term "learning" implies a more formal and conscious process. As a social studies teacher of a mainstream class with ELL students, your curriculum promotes the acquisition of the English language through the learning of social studies content. So, successful communication with English language learners involves two components: (a) modified input and (b) modified interaction. This chapter focuses primarily on modifying input with visual support and on teaching strategies to assist ELL students in comprehending course content, as well as in developing proficiency in English. Chapter 2 explained how to modify interaction and provided an overview of important linguistic issues that should be understood prior to considering the teaching strategies offered in this chapter.

## How can I help the ELL students develop greater proficiency in English?

Without major changes in the way you teach and with minor modifications in the way you communicate, you can guide ELL students to develop English proficiency and to perform better in your social studies class. As a teacher, your own understanding of cultural values, intercultural communications, and learning styles will serve as a base in assisting you to do this. In maintaining high expectations for all students, you may decide to carefully choose specific content topics that are motivating and pertinent to the overall lesson, such as guiding your students to specific vocabulary or bolded words prior to assigning a chapter reading, asking them to describe the pictures in the chapter, providing a list of specific topics, or assigning students to use the Internet to explore the chapter topic. In this way, you will avoid the need for specific high literacy skills that your ELL students may not have at this point and provide a knowledge base on the upcoming chapter. For example, in teaching a lesson on the Civil War, providing an outline of the events in a chapter will give ELL students a preliminary focus for class discussions and readings. Also, taking the time to search for or ask your media specialist to locate other readings on the Civil War at the ELL students' mastery level will promote more opportunities for involvement in class discussions.

It is imperative to modify your spoken language to meet the needs of your ELL students at various levels. Some simple but essential strategies are to paraphrase main ideas consistently, repeat key points often, and check for comprehension frequently. Involving your students in varied activities using a buddy and providing lots of media and realia will also support English language development. Since you should use English at a level conducive to your ELL students' abilities, other strategies such as scaffolding, thematic instruction, group work, and the SDAIE model (see below, p. 24) may prove to be effective in your social studies classroom.

A scaffold, or temporary support structure, is a useful technique until your ELL students become proficient enough to comprehend the material. For example, when presenting to your elementary students the sailing adventures of Columbus to the New World, provide a list of the ships (*Santa Maria, Niña, Pinta*), the coasts and areas traveled, and any other pertinent vocabulary terms; review the grammar structures in the text prior to a reading assignment so that you present any challenging grammatical structures, such as verb tense, adjectives, or adverbs to your ELL students; or incorporate a group activity for students to work collaboratively in understanding the readings, such as a map or computer activity. Your overall goal is to challenge ELL students while at the same time providing encouragement, assistance, support, and guidance so that they may acquire the content without a language barrier.

Another simple way to create a strong English base and at the same time build connections among social studies topics is to incorporate thematic lessons. Group activities provide ELL students the opportunity to listen to and speak more English, to repeat vocabulary, paraphrase as needed, have more control of their usage of English, clarify any misunderstandings, and lower their anxiety and stress in the classroom.

The Specially Designed Academic Instruction in English (SDAIE) model is an effective technique that focuses on the lesson content, comprehension strategies, connections with ELL students' own experiences, and classroom interaction.[2] For example, a lesson on the "Power of Compounding" in an elementary classroom might look something like this:

## Content Objective
- To determine the value of your money if you put it in a savings account.

## Language Objectives
- To comprehend vocabulary related to American money (dollars, cents, quarters, dimes, nickels, pennies).
- To express comparative quantities (more than, less than, equal, etc.).

## Lesson Activities
The teacher provides students with paper coins and dollars and the students determine how much money they would like to save in their fictitious class bank accounts, and how much interest their savings will earn. Everyone is given a bankbook and the class determines the structure of how to earn paper dollars in the classroom, i.e., working cooperatively in groups earns 25 cents, following class rules earns 50 cents, etc. Students actively participate in discussions and practice determining interest rates through your modeling, interactions with each other, and frequent comprehension checks.

## Connections
ELL students share their cultures' monetary system with the class, maybe even bringing in samples of the currency. Then, the teacher connects the importance of saving money to the students' personal desires to buy certain items such as toys, games, software, etc.

## Interaction
A class store is established for the students to earn paper dollars on a regular basis and purchase items. This provides for lots of conversation, role-plays, and opportunities for your ELL students to use the English language.

The SDAIE model is a unique opportunity enabling ELL students to master the English language and grammar at an appropriate grade level without formal instruction in English. With careful guidance, ELL students will be better able to understand the primary focus of your lessons.

There are two other well-known models of teaching subject matter content to ELL students that warrant mention here. They both are used primarily in "sheltered" classes (those that include only English language learners), and direct the lessons' pitch and pace to their specific language development levels. Because this book focuses on including ELL students in the mainstream social studies classroom, we have emphasized an instructional approach, the Natural Approach, which can more effectively integrate ELL teaching strategies with those geared toward native speakers. In any case, for readers who will be involved in developing curriculum and instruction specifically for ELL students in sheltered settings, we recommend review of the Cognitive Academic Language Learning Approach,[3] also known as CALLA, and the Sheltered Instruction Observation Protocol, also known as the SIOP.[4]

### How can I help ELL students comprehend complex concepts that require strong verbal skills?
Useful techniques such as graphic organizers, semantic mapping, realia, time lines, political cartoons, and resources like visual dictionaries, videos, and CD ROMs can be beneficial to all students. (Extended discussion and examples of specific learning activities appropriate for K-12 social studies classrooms will be addressed in Part II). Being flexible in your choice of techniques and resources will give your ELL students more choices in learning about social studies themes and lesson topics.

After studying the American Revolutionary War, an elementary teacher may ask her students to draw a picture to depict something important or meaningful about the war. She then laminates the pictures and forms a class "quilt" or timeline that she hangs in her room. This activity can lead to lots of class interaction and opportunities for ELL students who might not have a strong English background. Use "verbal markers" such as words like "now," "next," "first," "second," "then," and "finally," to focus ELL students strategically on the topic. Support these verbal markers with nonverbal cues such as using your fingers to denote first, second, etc.

Another option for assisting ELL students who lack strong verbal skills in English is to use the SQ4R model of Survey, Question, Read, Reflect, Recite, and Review.[5] ELL students scan the chapter focusing on bold words, headings, or subheadings; read the chapter and reflect on their previous experiences based on the topic; review questions and re-read to better comprehend the lesson. As a social studies teacher, you may choose to select a topic that you feel would be more motivating for your ELL students and not follow the sequential order in the chapter index of the text.

Another way to support ELL students is to tailor the material to fit their English language level. For example, in presenting early explorers in America from 1510-1542 such as Balboa, Cortes, DeVaca, DeSoto, and Coronado, allow ELL students to focus on a single explorer and become knowledgeable about this one person.

Keep in mind that ELL students who tend to be "silent" in class may do so because of cultural differences and not because they do not know the answer. For example, silence is sometimes a symbol of respect for Asian students. A mistake in class by a Korean student could be taken as a personal embarrassment. Thus, good teaching strategies, language modifications, and an understanding of other cultures are all necessary to work collectively with your students. Complex concepts must be delivered at a level conducive to the ELL students' abilities and this takes extra effort by social studies teachers.

### What are some proven, effective strategies for teaching social studies to ELL students?

Among the most effective strategies is to provide students with a high degree of contextual support. Jim Cummins developed an easily understood and widely used model for providing contextual support and helping students successfully complete cognitively demanding academic tasks.[6] He defined everyday language conversation as Basic Interpersonal Communication (BICS) and proficiency in using the language in the classroom as Cognitive Academic Language Proficiency (CALP). His model has two distinct dimensions to distinguish conversational from academic language: (1) the level of contextual support such as maps, visuals, gestures, clues, etc. and (2) the degree of cognitive demand, which refers to the level of difficulty of the task or topic for the ELL student.

| I<br>Low Cognitive Demand and High Context<br>*(The easiest quadrant to master)* | III<br>High Cognitive Demand and High Context |
|---|---|
| II<br>Low Cognitive Demand and Low Context | IV<br>High Cognitive Demand and Low Context<br>*(The most difficult quadrant to master.)* |

In the primary grades students tend to learn content through contextual support (Quadrants I and III); however, instruction in grades 3-12 requires more cognitive academic proficiency tasks such as comparing, contrasting, and explaining, and there is less contextual support (Quadrants II and IV). Social studies teachers should continually remind themselves that their course content requires a high level of literacy and more cognitively demanding tasks. In order to be successful in teaching, an awareness of both language dimensions (level of contextual support and degree of cognitive demand) is essential in implementing effective lessons for all students.

Here is an example of an effective strategy to contextualize the subject for ELL students when planning a lesson on the American Revolutionary War:

1. The teacher begins with an activity such as a KWL Chart (Know/Want to Know/Learn) to elicit what students already know, what they want to know, and what they would like to learn. Students who have schema regarding the American Revolutionary War share their knowledge, which will help build a base for those who have no previous background. Once students have expressed their background knowledge, the teacher highlights key concepts, words, and events by writing them on the board and checking for comprehension. The ELL students can look up the words in their bilingual dictionaries and follow up by consulting with a bilingual aide.

2. As an expansion of KWL, ELL students at higher levels of English proficiency can share any information they know regarding the history of revolutions in their native

countries. This connects their schema regarding political revolutions to the topic of the lesson, and it expands other students' knowledge of world history and perspectives.

3. Once students' background knowledge is brought to the forefront, the teacher should immerse students in contextualized, experiential activities, using props, role-plays, maps/graphs, and other means of non-verbal support. A good rule of thumb is that if students can simply listen to your voice and not miss much, then you need to add more context for your ELL students.

4. Through intermittent cooperative learning activities, the ELL students can further build their schema and can clarify questions that they may feel intimidated to address to the entire class. For example, once the teacher has presented a topic to the class, students can pair up, review their notes, and re-state the main points to one another. In cases where ELL students are at the beginning stage of English proficiency, they can benefit from hearing the main points summarized by a native speaker whom they can question for clarification and deeper understanding. When ELL students are at a higher level of proficiency, having the opportunity to re-state the main points to a native speaker not only helps them comprehend the subject but also helps them develop their English skills.

### How do I modify my questioning and discussion techniques for ELL students?

So often we hear: "I've studied Spanish for three years but they talk so fast it's hard to understand." Remembering the "V.I.P.S." in speaking to students is a key factor. "V" stands for the quality and pitch of your voice in talking with students individually versus as a whole class. So often we witness teachers raising their voices to gain the ELL students' attention, when in fact, the ELL has no clue what the teacher is even saying. "I" is for intonation in properly enunciating key words and phrases; "P" stands for pausing to allow students to comprehend what is said and think about a response; and "S" is for speed in producing sentences and in giving students time to process the language.

> **V**: voice—quality and pitch
> **I**: intonation—proper enunciation
> **P**: pausing—for comprehension and response
> **S**: speed—giving time to process the language

In establishing questioning techniques, researchers such as Rita and Kenneth Dunn have demonstrated the effectiveness of asking a question, pausing, calling on a student, and pausing again before providing feedback on the response (or lack of response).[7] Simple tips such as avoiding lots of contractions, pronouns, and idioms will provide for clearer communication, as will simple vocabulary words and non-verbals. Another modification that will prove to be quite beneficial to your students is the use of "caretaker speech" in which smaller functional words (i.e., the, an, of, on, in, etc.) are de-emphasized in comparison to the nouns and verbs in the sentence structure. Of course, the usual "good teaching" practices of repetition, rephrasing, and checking for comprehension are also beneficial. Bilingual dictionaries are an essential tool, as is allowing an ELL student to use a script to support an oral presentation.

Another effective strategy for modifying discussion techniques is to use the Language Experience Approach (LEA) in which students are encouraged to express their understanding in their own words. For example, after reading a selected chapter, students brainstorm a list of the main ideas and the teacher writes this information on the board. Students are then asked to work in small groups to form a story using these main ideas. Each group reads its story aloud. This provides lots of interaction and opportunities for ELL students to add in their personal comments in building the story. Another strategy is the Direct Reading Thinking Activity (DR-TA) in which students make predictions on a given topic, then read about the topic. This too allows the ELL students to refer to their previous learning experiences and knowledge prior to attempting to read the chapter. It is an opportunity for the social studies teacher to present any challenging vocabulary terms, themes, or essential facts in the reading as well.

### How do I assess ELL students' progress in my social studies classroom? What modifications in evaluation strategies should I make?

Specific modifications must be made to subject area tests to enable ELL students to demonstrate their mastery of the topic. This may include oral reading of the test, clarification of vocabulary words, demonstration of the instructions accompanying the test, visual representation of concepts and/or vocabulary, highlighting or underlining essential vocabulary on the test, and providing bilingual dictionaries. Of course, asking a bilingual teacher or ESOL specialist to proctor the test is an excellent option, but one that is not always available.

Grading the work of ELL students is also challenging, as content knowledge is your major focus, not English language skills. Teachers often give a pass/fail grade for lower level English language learners or grade more leniently to encourage future studying and interest in social studies. Multiple-choice items can be more difficult to master due to the low reading abilities of some ELL students. Thus, designing a test using fill-in-the-blank strategies, word banks, cloze-ended questions (in which the teacher omits key words or phrases in a passage), or even providing for an open-book test are effective strategies for ELL students at all levels. Other options to assess progress include allowing ELL students the opportunity to develop a "portfolio" based on a given unit of study; student simulations; reenactments of an historical or political event, and multimedia presentations. It is important to assess students frequently and to provide positive feedback as often as possible. Assessment does not have to be in the form of the traditional paper-and-pencil test. Observations, interviews, and informal testing measures can be viable means of assessing an ELL student's learning. The National Clearinghouse for English Language Acquisition has designed seven principles for assessing ELL students and we have adapted them into the following five categories to fit the needs of social studies teachers:[8]

1. In assessing your ELL students' understanding of social studies, include their unique characteristics in an appropriate manner, i.e., avoid cultural bias and provide word banks or pictures when basic English vocabulary is lacking.
2. Assess their knowledge in social studies based on their language proficiency and comprehension level, i.e., if you have covered four historical leaders but due to low proficiency in English you allowed your ELL to focus on one leader, then test your ELL on solely one leader.
3. Design a challenging yet appropriate assessment based on high standards to provide you with valid information for making decisions on your ELL students' status.
4. Your assessment should be designed to accommodate the ELL students' levels of language comprehension so that you may make informed decisions based on the results of the tests, i.e., if you require extensive reading in your test and your ELL students are at a beginning level of proficiency in reading, then their scores will not match their understanding of the social studies content.
5. Evaluate their comprehension through multiple types of assessments, i.e., portfolios, observations, group activities, projects, etc.

Overall, the consistent monitoring of your ELL students' progress academically and in English proficiency with an array of strategies is pivotal to providing an accurate and meaningful record. Even a self-assessment checklist is a viable technique to use as another option for assessing your ELL students' progress in the classroom. Maintaining a low anxiety assessment process will assist ELL students tremendously, as will more flexible time limitations in testing.

### How can I use cooperative learning effectively in my social studies class if one or some of the students are ELL students?

More than 500 empirical research studies show that cooperative learning improves mastery of content, social skills development, and collaboration in the classroom. Emerging investigations conclude that cooperative learning may also be an effective way of combating and reducing prejudice. In culturally diverse classrooms, collaborative education may be one way to foster positive ethnic relations. It is also useful in helping to develop ELL students' proficiency, particularly in the area of CALP. Both homogeneous and heterogeneous groupings (i.e., by level of achievement, English proficiency, or native language) and the "buddy system" are also effective strategies.

Although social studies seems to go hand-in-hand with cooperative learning strategies, it is more challenging because of its highly abstract and language-dependent topics. Students with a limited English vocabulary of 500 words mixed with those who can comprehend approximately 12,000 words, along with students proficient in English, provide a complex setting for any social studies teacher. The need to maintain a respectful, communicative, and productive group situation is quite challenging. One suggestion is to use Elliott Aaronson's "jigsaw" technique, in which students are put into groups and each student is assigned a specific topic to become an "expert" in a given area.[9] After reading about and studying the given topic, the experts from each group come together to share their findings prior to sharing with their own group. For example, after forming groups of five students, you assign each student in that group one of the following Americans: Alexander Graham Bell, Francis Scott Key, John Paul Jones, Alexander Hamilton, Harriet Beecher Stowe. The students investigate their famous American on their own. You provide your ELL students with a famous American who you feel would lead to much success in researching, as there might be material available in your classroom, in the media center, or in reading books on an easier level to comprehend.

Affording time for your ELL students to meet with other students who have investigated the same famous American allows for more interaction and enables both academic content and English proficiency to be gained. Your ELL students could choose to present their information through a *PowerPoint* presentation, pictures, graphs, or verbally with a script.

Incorporating cooperative learning techniques with ELL students is challenging, but with careful planning you will see the positive effects on the students. If after presenting an economics lesson to your high school students, you asked them to design a news broadcast based on an economic perspective, this would provide multiple opportunities for all students to participate based on academic and language proficiency. ELL students succeed in a mainstream classroom especially when proper modeling and reinforcement is presented in a positive and encouraging manner. Cooperative learning techniques assist in this process.

### How do I determine the appropriateness of the classroom textbook and how can I support ELL students' comprehension of the reading content?

By some estimates, the textbook is the most consulted educational resource in the social studies classroom, even more so than the classroom teacher. It stands to reason, then, that a course textbook should be examined to assess the appropriateness of its language and to determine the amount and type of support ELL students need to work successfully with it. An analysis of vocabulary and sentence structure can reveal how the text should be modified and simplified. Keep in mind the overall structure and design for your ELL students, i.e., a concise index on chapter topics, a glossary of terms included in the text, chapter summaries or even frequent summaries in each chapter, questions elicited prior to and at the end of the chapter, chapter lengths that are conducive to all proficiency levels, bold wording of key concepts, clear pictures to support readings, accurate graphics, length of paragraphs reasonable for ELL students at all levels, review sections, and even a section specifically designed to aid ELL students' comprehension. Also, highlighting key terms, encouraging the use of bilingual dictionaries, and providing an overview on the board or overhead of the main topics in the chapter

will be beneficial for all students. In some cases, you may find a similar text at a lower level of reading proficiency for your ELL to master the content knowledge. Merely pointing out the glossary or review page in each chapter can be a simple but strategic idea for promoting ELL students' success in using the text.

Another innovative strategy that has proven to be quite successful in supporting ELL students' comprehension of the text reading is the "Teach the Text Backward" technique.[10] Here you ask your students to share their knowledge of the chapter topic prior to a reading assignment. For example, if you were going to read about the economic status of the Western world, you would begin by asking your students to share their thoughts and ideas on this topic. Guide them through a series of pre-developed questions based on the chapter reading. Then, briefly review, and answer if possible, the questions at the end of the text chapter. Finally ask students to read the chapter. So often with the given time restrictions and overwhelming curriculum, teachers assign a reading, get students to answer the comprehension questions at the end of the chapter, follow up with class discussions, and then allow students to make personal connections with the reading topic. In using the "Teach the Text Backward" approach, this is done in the exact opposite format to allow ELL students to personalize the information, become motivated to read about it in English, and to have a clear focus on the reading topic. It also allows ELL students to share their cultural experiences as they relate to the topic and feel more a part of class discussions.

### What types of adaptations in curricular materials should I make?

Social studies teachers often incorporate outside resources into their classrooms. These include trade books, primary documents, newspaper articles, videos, ready-made printed materials, and computer software, which provide opportunities for analysis and synthesis as well as an enriching experience. However, care must be taken that materials are at appropriate reading levels, free from cultural bias, and clearly provide multiple perspectives. It is especially beneficial if the materials focus on the native cultures and languages of your ELL students to promote more involvement and communication in the classroom.

Another effective tool for adapting your materials is to tape the chapter readings so that ELL students may listen to the tape while following along with the text. Perhaps you have honors students or classroom assistants who could read aloud and tape themselves so that you have a tape for each chapter reading done by an array of student voices.

## How can technology support progress in English as well as the comprehension of social studies content?

Bilingual software, visual representations (still and video), student centers or stations, and specialized software can be dynamic and motivating tools for ELL students. With forethought, social studies teachers can fashion learning activities using the Internet and have ELL students complete research on a given topic. An exciting and innovative approach to making the content come alive is to provide a virtual field trip, e.g., connect to a history museum website to enliven class discussions and readings.

Using videos is a fascinating way for ELL students to get a picture of the content being studied, but it does not always mean that the student understands what is said on the video. An outline of the video content or prior questions would serve as a beneficial teaching tool in using videos in the classroom.

Overall, Computer-Assisted Language Learning (CALL) is a viable option for increasing student involvement in and comprehension of the social studies lessons. The mechanisms available to students for editing grammar, and spelling, and for translating, along with the innovative means of creating a *PowerPoint* presentation, and the ease of communicating with peers through e-mail and instant messaging are all tools to support academic and language proficiency. For example, if you are studying Australia, what better way to present the lesson than through real-life pictures and scenes from Australia? These pictures can be used in a *PowerPoint* demonstration or viewed through websites and Internet resources. Fortunately, social studies textbooks now provide numerous websites to support the lesson topics. More accurate comprehension of your lesson will be possible if students use technology to search for lesson topics at a more appropriate reading level. If you have the time to find a few beneficial sites that seem to be geared toward students who read below grade level, this will be an excellent addition to your overall curriculum. If not, ELL students can be guided into finding information either in their own languages or at a more appropriate level.

Another supporting technological activity is to ask ELL students to show the class scenes and sites from their homelands. Again, this will allow the ELL to feel more invited and welcomed into the American classroom and motivate others to learn more about the culture of their peers.

## What types of support personnel are available to help me in my classroom?

In today's mainstream classroom there are numerous possible options for personnel support. Some schools provide a bilingual aide to work with teachers and students. This aide can be quite beneficial if she or he can speak the language of the ELL student; however, if the aide is not fluent, this makes for a more challenging situation.

ESOL specialists are also available at some schools, especially where there is a high population of ELL students. Since Hispanic students are the dominant English language learners in most schools (Hispanic students comprise approximately 75 percent of ELL students nationwide), a bilingual aide is often on hand to support teachers and students. This aide may come into your classroom and work directly with ELL students or may pull out the students to work together on a routine schedule. Another alternative for obtaining support personnel is to check with your social studies supervisor, as this individual may have training in ESOL methods. Currently in some states, such as Florida, college students in early childhood, elementary, English, and special education will graduate by 2004 from an approved education program with an ESOL endorsement. Thus, these teachers will be beneficial to all students and teachers. They will have had the training and some field experience in directly teaching and assessing ELL students.

Also, students in your own classroom may be the most supportive means of assisting you with ELL students at a very low proficiency level. Students can translate for others, assist with directions, interpret when necessary to get your message conveyed accurately, and check for comprehension. We all know that students learn well from each other and thus your best course of action might be sitting in your own classroom! A word of caution on using same language buddies is needed, however. While in general it is a good strategy, we must remember that the more proficient ELL buddies may not know academic, discipline-specific terms in their native language unless they have studied them in either a bilingual program or in their native countries. For example, they may have learned the term "checks and balances" in an English social studies lesson, but they may not know the term in their native languages and thereby cannot effectively translate it for the new ELL student. More proficient buddies can help a new student a great deal, especially in feeling welcome and understanding classroom procedures. In many cases they may also help them understand content through translation, but we must not depend on this as the sole means of ensuring that the new ELL student comprehends concepts and terms. Lastly, using the resources in the community, such as parent volunteers, cultural organizations, and library resources will also prove to be beneficial in providing more support for you and your ELL students.

### Notes

1. Stephen D. Krashen, *The Input Hypothesis: Issues and Implications* (Harlow: Longman, 1981).

2. California State Department of Education, *Schooling and Language Minority Students: A Theoretical Framework* (Los Angeles: Evaluation, Dissemination and Assessment Center, California State University, 1994).

3. Anna U. Chamot and J. Michael O'Malley, *The CALLA Handbook: Implementing the Cognitive Academic Language Learning Approach* (Reading, MA: Addison-Wesley, 1994).

4. Deborah J. Short and Jana Echevarria, *The Sheltered Instruction Observation Protocol: A Tool for Teacher-Researcher Collaboration and Professional Development* (ERIC Digest Online at http://www.cal.org/ericcll/digest/sheltered.html, Retrieved: February 28, 2003).

5. E.L. Thomas and H.A. Robinson, *Improved Reading in Every Class: A Sourcebook for Teachers* (Boston: Allyn and Bacon, 1972).

6. Jim Cummins, *Negotiating Identities: Education for Empowerment in a Diverse Society* (Los Angeles: California Association for Bilingual Education, 1996).

7. Rita and Kenneth Dunn, *Teaching Secondary Students Through Individual Learning Styles: Practical Approaches for Grades 7-12* (Boston: Allyn & Bacon, 1993).

8. National Clearinghouse for English Language Acquisition (NCELA), *Assessment Standards for English Language Learners.* Retrieved March 10, 2003 at http://www.ncela.gwu.edu/ncbepubs/assessmentstandards/execsum/execsummary.pdf

9. See Elliot Aaronson, *The Jigsaw Classroom* (Beverly Hills, CA: Sage, 1978).

10. Judith Jameson, *Enriching Content Classes for Secondary ESOL Students* (McHenry, IL: Delta Systems, 1998).

# CHAPTER 4
# Celebrating Cultural and Linguistic Diversity

## How can I make my ELL students feel more included and welcomed in my classroom?

Assisting students to feel like contributing participants in the learning community is the first step in developing their academic proficiency and fostering their desire to learn a new language. In doing so, providing a classroom environment where ELL students feel comfortable, safe, and secure is pivotal to helping them develop their English language skills and at the same time comprehend the social studies curriculum. Simple strategies and techniques include:

1. Learning to correctly pronounce the names of your ELL students;
2. Sending a letter home to parents in their native language on class expectations and policies, major topics, projects, etc.;
3. Providing a visual for class routines with a picture to depict each routine;
4. Inviting ELL students to make a presentation about their culture to the entire class. If their English proficiency is low, or if they decline, assign more proficient students to investigate the cultures of your beginning ELL students and to present the information to the class;
5. Providing clear directions verbally, following up with written directions on the board and modeling of directions;
6. Labeling items in the classroom in the languages of your ELL students and in English;
7. Setting high expectations for all students with an understanding that it is a language barrier that often impedes instruction and not an academic one;
8. Checking continuously for comprehension by asking for simple one word responses, asking yes/no questions, and making true/false statements;
9. Assigning ELL students to an English speaking classmate; and
10. Monitoring your classroom structure so that you place ELL students in the middle or in front of the room, where they will have your attention and you will have many opportunities for frequent eye contact and interaction.

These simple class ideas will assist ELL students to learn new vocabulary, encourage cross-cultural simulations, and engender good will in the classroom community. With the goal being to welcome ELL students in the classroom and build upon their language fluency in English along with academic understanding, social studies teachers must also be cognizant of the topics that may offend the various cultures represented in their classrooms.

Lily W. Fillmore and Catherine E. Snow's categories of teachers provide another way of looking at yourself and assisting your ELL students to feel more included and welcomed in your classroom.[1] You are a "communicator" with your students, colleagues, administrators, parents and community; you serve as an "educator, evaluator, and agent of socialization" and you are an educated human being who aspires to promote a positive attitude in your classroom. Reconfirming your role will promote effective teaching in the multicultural, diverse classroom of the twenty-first century. Through your consistent class policies and your awareness of cultural differences, ELL students will adapt to your class setting.

A bulletin board highlighting your ELL students' cultures is a welcoming suggestion, as is a list of recommended websites where students can check out information regarding the cultures of their classmates. Finally, keeping lines of communication open between you and your ELL students and their parents is a sure way to provide a welcoming and inviting classroom. Taking the time to send home updates, weekly assignments, or class news in the ELL students' languages (if possible) will allow for more interaction and involvement of the ELL students, parents, and community. Sonia Nieto researched how teachers have been successful in working with culturally and linguistically diverse students.[2] Her list includes teachers who place a high value on students' identities (culture, race, language, gender, experiences), make the connections between students' lives and learning, create a safe classroom environment, engage in active learning strategies, look at themselves as lifelong learners, and demonstrate care and respect for all students. As Nieto so clearly reports, it is essential to keep in mind that teachers consciously and unconsciously bring their own values into the classroom.[3] They bring their "autobiographies" such as experiences, identities, values, beliefs, attitudes, hang-ups, biases, wishes, dreams and more. In welcoming ELL students into your classroom, it is important to be aware of your own "autobiography" to effectively facilitate academic learning and English proficiency.

### How can I make my ELL students feel valued in my social studies classroom?

Successful social studies teachers can capitalize on the experiences and backgrounds of their ELL students by incorporating their cultures and languages into their lessons. Simple strategies such as "Word of the Week" (a new vocabulary word from the ELL student's home language) will not only help the ELL feel valued within the classroom community, but can also impart new skills and knowledge to the entire class. Other strategies, such as dual language support, are more labor intensive but can be highly effective. In this way, both the native language(s) of the ELL students and the English language are used to present the main concepts of the lesson. If there are numerous ELL students from the same heritage, have them work together to present an aspect of the lesson from their culture. For example, in presenting a lesson on American explorers, the ELL students could also share information about famous explorers from their culture so that their heritage becomes part of the class discussion as well. In trying to make ELL students feel valued in your social studies class, Douglas Brown's criteria of culturally appropriate techniques should prove quite beneficial: [4]

1. Recognize the values and belief systems of all students, including your ELL students.
2. Draw on background experiences of your ELL students.
3. Recognize that not all cultures actively participate in class discussions, i.e., Asian students do not tend to shout out an answer or raise their hands even if they know the answer; Native Americans are usually not asked to read aloud in class.
4. Empathetically and tactfully present materials that might go beyond the comfort zones of the cultures represented by your ELL students.
5. Be aware of gender roles in different cultures.
6. Refrain from demeaning stereotypes of any culture.

Values unconsciously permeate class feelings, attitudes, and lessons. As a social studies teacher you have your own set of values about classroom procedures, academic activities, classroom organization, homework, testing, parental communication, student expectations, and grading. Your values are key to supporting the values of ELL students in that they will affect all students' learning. Tracking ELL students as low or non-academic, and designing a curriculum omitting ELL students' cultures will devalue the feelings and attitudes in your classroom. There seems to be enough pressure placed on covering curriculum and preparing students for standardized tests; yet a focus on student values is as essential in promoting academic and social success.

A typical mainstream American classroom is a place where students follow a set schedule, actively participate in routines, maintain discipline, conform to authority, and strive to achieve academically in order to preserve their self worth.[5] Allow your ELL students to feel more valued and welcomed in your social studies classroom, by maintaining an overall awareness of the cultural, social and academic differences in educational systems.

### In what ways can I incorporate my ELL students' cultures and experiences into my social studies classroom?

As a social studies teacher, your curriculum lends itself to an array of opportunities for ELL students to share their personal experiences and knowledge based on their cultures. Their cultural and linguistic backgrounds can be used to teach social studies content in a variety of ways. For instance, ask your ELL students to be leaders of a research team that investigates their own culture, establish debate teams, design compare/contrast activities with American lifestyles, have show-and-tell of one's own culture, show cultural videos, and continuously research the news and culture of your ELL students.

Another strategy to make ELL students feel valued is the use of Culture Capsules and Culture Assimilators to promote positive cultural understanding. The Culture Capsule was originally designed by Taylor and Sorenson in 1961 and is still used today as an effective strategy to present one specific difference between American and other cultures in important areas of life, such as government, religion, economics, schools, etc. This class activity can be done in ten minutes. Either you or your students write a brief description of a cultural perspective, followed by a list of comprehension questions and a class activity. Below is an example of a culture capsule on restaurants in the U.S.A.

## Culture Capsule: American Restaurants

In the United States, "eating out" or "going out to eat" is a popular way of sharing meals with family and friends. Home cooking in America has decreased greatly over the past twenty years due to the change in lifestyles of American families and to the number of mothers who work outside the home. Americans tend to enjoy restaurants that are conveniently located near their homes. Restaurants offering affordable prices for the average American are easily found. Popular restaurants include American grilles, bar-b-ques, sports bars, and fast food establishments such as McDonald's and Burger King. Even some ethnic restaurants (e.g., Chinese, Mexican, Thai, or Japanese) have become Americanized using popular U.S. cooking styles.

The "fast foods" are the most convenient and affordable options. McDonald's, which originated in California in the 1950s, serves the typical American hamburger, cheeseburger, and french fries. It increased its fast-paced style to "drive-thru" in the 1970s so people can just drive up to a window, order, pay, pick up their meal, and leave within five minutes! Eating on the run is very common for Americans, as is ordering take-out food to eat while watching television at home. Other typical fast food restaurants include Burger King (hamburgers and french fries), Kentucky Fried Chicken or KFC (fried chicken), Taco Bell (tacos and burritos), Arby's (roast beef sandwiches), Boston Market ("home style" foods), and Subway (sandwiches).

It is typical to drive through American cities or small towns and see a plethora of fast food restaurants. American grille or "bistro" type restaurants are also very popular. These are often called "chain restaurants" as they are franchised, or sold to local owners and offer the same menu and décor regardless of location. American foods consist of appetizers or "finger foods" such as nachos, fried chicken fingers, onion rings, cheese sticks, and mushrooms. Popular entrees are salads with chicken or meat, soups, sandwiches, steaks, an array of fish, turkey, pork, and ham. Some popular American grills or bistros are Bennigan's, Hops, Chili's, Outback Steakhouse, and T.G.I. Friday's.

Class Questions
1. What American foods do you like to eat?
2. What are your experiences with American restaurants?
3. When do you eat out?
4. If you could own a restaurant in America, what kind of food would you offer?

Materials
Menus from American restaurants
Internet sites on restaurants

Activity
Practice ordering foods from the menus
Set up a field trip to a restaurant
Write a recipe for a favorite food from your culture.

Many years ago, social psychologists developed the Culture Assimilator to facilitate the transition to living in a foreign culture.[6] Basically, it provides a brief description of a cross-cultural interaction that leads to a misunderstanding between an American and a target culture. After the description of the incident, students are presented with four plausible explanations from which to choose the correct response. If they choose the wrong one, they are encouraged to continue to read on and discover the one accurate choice. Unlike the Culture Capsule, this may be a silent reading activity. An example of a misunderstanding is given below.

## Culture Assimilator: Bargaining

Juanita has just arrived from Guatemala to her new American high school. Her classmate Ann, who is in most of her classes, greets her. They take a tour of the school and Ann talks about living in the U.S.

After a few weeks, Juanita tells Ann how difficult it is for her family to get around town without a car and that they will be shopping for one that weekend. Ann seizes the moment to explain how to bargain for a car in America and how to talk with the car sales manager. At first Juanita is confused, but after Ann shares the story of how her father bought a car below the sticker price, Juanita seems much more confident in purchasing a car. That weekend, Juanita's family purchases a used car and Juanita is very successful in using her bargaining skills to make the final sale.

The next week, Juanita's mother wants to purchase some furniture and Juanita goes shopping with her mother with the intent of bargaining for the right price! Juanita's mother finds the perfect sofa. Just as Juanita approaches the saleswoman, her friend Ann comes over and tries to explain that this is not appropriate in a furniture store. However, Juanita wants to show her friend how she can barter and begins to bargain for a lower price. The situation escalates and Juanita and her mother are asked to leave the store. Ann is very embarrassed as she tries desperately to explain the proper way to purchase furniture, but Juanita is very insistent. Ann leaves the store quickly and Juanita is quite confused.

Which response do you feel is more appropriate?
a. Foreigners should not attempt to bargain with Americans.
b. Only certain items are negotiable in America.
c. Since the salesperson at the car dealership knew that Juanita's family was new to the area, he was willing to make a deal on the car.
d. Juanita tried to bargain too low for the sofa and this was not acceptable.

If you chose…
(a) Salespeople in the United States are generally interested in making a sale to anybody, including foreigners. Try again.
(b) This is the correct answer. While it is common to negotiate the price on certain goods and services in America, most items have a fixed price.
(c) At the car dealership Juanita just used her immigrant status as a bargaining tool. There is a more accurate answer—keep trying.
(d) When negotiating a price in America (for a house or car, for example), it is not considered bad practice to go lower than the other person will accept. In fact, this is part of the normal process. Look for a more appropriate response.

Both the Culture Capsule and Assimilator may be designed to fit the curricula topics in your social studies classroom. You may design your own scenarios or ask students to develop them. Either way, both strategies enable you to incorporate American culture and the cultures and experiences of your ELL students into your classroom.

## What can I do to foster positive home-school-community relations?

Positive relations between home and school are a critical factor for all students' success. As a social studies teacher, you are already aware of the need to learn as much as possible about the cultures represented in your classroom, establish and maintain communication with the home, and foster collaboration with your students' parents and/or caregivers. Parents play a crucial role in supporting the academic achievement of your students. Even though most parents place a high value on education and have a great interest in the success of their children in school, not all parents become involved in the educational experiences of their children. Teachers and administrators must work together to create favorable conditions for communicating with families and encourage them to take an active role in the education of their children. This is particularly important for English language learners who need extra reinforcement, encouragement, and support from their teachers and their families due to the cultural and linguistic differences they may be experiencing.

As part of your role, taking on the responsibility to encourage parental involvement is a very effective strategy to support your students' achievement and overall success.

However, the biggest obstacle is "time" away from your academic responsibilities, just as it involves time from parents' work or family lives. For the parents of your ELL students, a language barrier is often tacked on to time constraints. It is therefore more challenging and cumbersome to foster home-school-community relations. Suggestions such as sending home newsletters in the native languages of ELL students, inviting parents to a school function with translators available, working with ELL community leaders to plan and offer a special informational event for parents of ELL students (e.g., understanding American school culture and expectations for parental support, understanding school board and school policies, such as dress code, and grading policies) planning a multicultural festival and asking for parental input and participation, and encouraging student-parent interaction in assignments are possible solutions to foster relationships.

M. Lee Manning and Leroy G. Baruth provide the following reasons for lack of parental involvement: [7] (a) language differences between home and school; (b) a belief on the part of parents that a child's difficulties in school reflect negatively on them; (c) a fear of disclosing personal and family problems that might cause family members to be seen in a negative light; (d) a distrust of teachers with different cultural backgrounds; (e) barriers created by parents' lack of understanding of the school system in the United States; and (f) parents' feelings of discomfort in the school setting.[8] With these in mind, and the cultural diversity of your subject area, an endless list of opportunities to overcome these barriers will become apparent as you design your curriculum. Perhaps assignments such as interviews, cultural backgrounds, ideological perspectives, Internet searches, personal experiences in other cultures, and more can be designed around student-parent involvement. For example, asking your students to trace their family heritage, or writing personal autobiographies will encourage parental involvement.

The more material you can send home in the native languages of ELL students, the more opportunities you provide for parental involvement. In addition to the student and teacher resources you have in your school, there are a number of computer programs and Internet sites that can translate from one language to another. Simple strategies such as sending home your class policies and expectations in the students' native languages will go a long way in fostering relations. Parents will appreciate your concerns and efforts, even if the grammar and spelling are imperfect. Upon completion of a chapter or unit, invite parents to attend your class to listen to students summarizing what they have learned. Provide lots of pictures and visuals for the non-English speaking parents. The opportunities abound if you take the time and initiative to foster parental involvement. Lastly, sending home a student journal or writing sample for a parent signature is a simple but strategic plan to involve parents.

### How can I encourage ELL students' parents to participate in my social studies classroom?

Although teachers seem to recognize the value of the participation of parents and other significant caregivers in the education of their children, teachers themselves may contribute to a lack of involvement. Teachers' lack of preparation for fostering parent involvement is one concern.[9] Another involves teacher attitudes, which include a lack of understanding of parents, misperceptions, and stereotypes. As Margaret Finders and Cynthia Lewis assert, "Too often, the social, economic, linguistic, and cultural practices of parents are represented as serious problems rather than valued knowledge."[10]

It is especially important for teachers to work toward understanding the cultural and linguistic backgrounds of ELL students. Severe problems may arise for students when their home cultures are not respected and valued in the school. Alma Flor Ada has written about the "profound inner conflicts" that students experience when they "discover the tremendous discrepancy between what the school proposes as accepted models and their own life experiences."[11] This situation also leaves parents feeling unable to make a contribution to their children's education.

The strong value and commitment to parental involvement among educators and the general public in the United States is apparent through many school activities and functions, such as PTA, School Advisory Committees, reading festivals, monthly parent meetings, school board meetings. There are volunteer opportunities in the school and in classrooms, where parents can assist classroom teachers by cutting, pasting, and making crafts at home, as well as for parents to participate in field trips. The link between higher student academic achievement and parental involvement has been clearly identified,[12] as has the link between student achievement and positive attitudes toward school.[13]

In sum, the parents or caregivers of ELL students who can provide reminiscences, offer demonstrations, or simply contribute realia and artifacts from their cultures provide parental input in the classroom. Teachers can send home invitations written in the home language encouraging parents to visit, observe, or contribute to the classroom community in myriad ways. Every teacher can create a list of opportunities for parents to actively participate in their children's education, especially in the elementary grades. As students move into their middle and high school years it becomes a little more challenging to be as active. However, numerous tips and strategies to welcome parents, community, and non-English speakers into your classroom have been provided. The challenge is now up to you to take the initiative and put forth the extra time to see it all happen. The rewards for you, your ELL students, parents, and community will far outweigh any time constraints.

## Notes

1. Lily W. Fillmore and Catherine E. Snow, *What Teachers Need to Know About Language.* [2000, online] Available: http://www.cal.org/ericcll/teachers/teachers.pdf [October 28, 2002].

2. Sonia Nieto, *What Keeps Teachers Going?* (New York: Teachers College Press, 2003).

3. *Ibid.*

4. H. Douglas Brown, *Principles of Language Learning and Teaching,* 4th Edition (New York: Addison Wesley Longman, Inc., 2000).

5. See the article by LeCompte in Lynne T. Diaz-Rico and Kathryn Z. Weed, *The Crosscultural, Language, and Academic Development Handbook: A Complete K-12 Reference Guide* (Boston: Allyn and Bacon, 2002).

6. Fred E. Fiedler, Terence Mitchell and Harry C. Triandis, "The Culture Assimilator: An Approach to Cross-Cultural Training," *Journal of Applied Psychology* 55, no. 2 (1971): 95-102.

7. M. Lee Manning and Leroy G. Baruth, *Multicultural Education of Children and Adolescents,* 3rd Edition (Boston: Allyn and Bacon, 2000).

8. Rebecca Constantino, L. Cui and C. Faltis, "Chinese Parental Involvement: Reaching New Levels," in *Equity and Excellence in Education* 28, no. 2 (1995): 46-50; Sanford M. Dornbusch and P. L. Ritter, "Parents of High School Students: A Neglected Resource," *Educational Horizons* 66 (1988): 75-77.

9. Joyce L. Epstein, *School, Family, and Community Partnerships: Preparing Educators and Improving Schools* (Boulder, CO: Westview Press, 2001); Gail L. Zellman, Brian Stecher, Stephen Klein and Daniel McCaffrey (with Silvia Gutierrez, Roger Madison, Denise D. Quigley, and Lisa Suarez), *Findings from an Evaluation of the Parent Institute for Quality Education Parent Involvement Program* (Rand Education, 1998), retrieved August 2, 2002, from http://www.rand.org/publications/MR/MR870/MR870.pdf

10. Margaret Finders and Cynthia Lewis, "Why Some Parents Don't Come to School," *Educational Leadership* 51, no. 8 (1994): 54.

11. Alma Flor Ada, "Preface," in Sudia Paloma McCaleb, *Building Communities of Learners: A Collaboration among Teachers, Students, Families, and Community* (Mahwah, NJ: Lawrence Erlbaum, 1997): vii.

12. Charles S. Clark, "Parents and Schools," *The CQ Researcher* (January 20, 1995). Retrieved August 2, 2002, from http://library.cqpress.com/cqres/lpext.dll/cqres/print/print1995120?print=yes

13. Christian J. Faltis, *Joinfostering: Teaching and learning in Multilingual Classrooms,* 3rd Edition (Upper Saddle River, NJ: Merrill/Prentice Hall, 2001).

# Part 2

# Teaching the Social Studies: Challenges and Prospects

# CHAPTER 5

# United States History

American History is a core component of any social studies curriculum. Whether ELL students were born in the United States or in another country, it is expected that they will be familiar with important historical events, people, and concepts. Students who come to the United States during their secondary school years have already been exposed to their country's history, and thus have a knowledge base that can be compared and contrasted with that of the United States. The focus of this chapter will be on helping the students become familiar with important historical figures, events, and concepts in American History, in line with the second theme of the social studies standards, ❶ **TIME, CONTINUITY, AND CHANGE**.

The results of the U.S. history assessment in the 2001 National Assessment of Educational Progress reported improvements in the average scores of 4th and 8th grade students since 1994.[1] Results for high school seniors were grim, however: Almost 60 percent of the nation's 12th graders lacked a basic knowledge of U.S. history.[2]

Fortunately, there are a number of strategies that can be used to facilitate the acquisition of historical knowledge and information in addition to regular tests—namely, the use of timelines, political cartoons, videos, and computer software. Alternative perspectives on key historical events (e.g., the Mexican-American War, the Vietnam War, and the Civil Rights Movement) can be enlightening for both ELL and mainstream students.

Since many ELL students or their parents have immigrated to the United States, one of the learning activities in this chapter helps students understand some of the "push" and "pull" factors that have made the U.S. such a pluralistic society. This topic will be extremely relevant to many ELL students and will allow them to share their own experiences regarding their emigration. This chapter will also utilize a role-playing strategy to teach about a key historical event at the turn of the twentieth century.

# Who's Who in American History

Students are inundated with symbols and references to important historical figures on a daily basis. From George Washington's face on every dollar bill, to political cartoons depicting Uncle Sam, it is important that ELL students be equipped with the knowledge needed to recognize and understand these references.

## Preproduction
At this stage, students will mostly listen as the teacher identifies important historical figures in American History by showing pictures.

## Materials
Fifteen to twenty sheets of blank notebook paper, pictures of U.S. symbols and of important contemporary and historical figures

## Strategy
1. Cut out fifteen to twenty pictures of U.S. symbols and of important figures in American History (e.g., political party symbols, Uncle Sam, George Washington, Abraham Lincoln, George W. Bush, Martin Luther King, Harriet Tubman).
2. Glue a picture on the front of a piece of paper and write the name and a simple phrase on the back of the paper, explaining for what the person is most noted.
3. Show the cards, one at a time, to the students and have them repeat the name of the person.
4. After doing this several times, the pages can be shuffled and you can ask students to demonstrate recall by pointing to the correct answer. You can also ask students to pronounce the terms after you.
5. When the students have become familiar with the names and pictures, the students can create cards of their own with names and simple descriptions and quiz each other in pairs.

## Extension Activity
Get a map of the city in which your school is located. After the students have become familiar with important historical names, have them peruse the map and see if any major streets, parks, or buildings are named after historical figures.

# Decisions, Decisions: What's in Your Trunk?

One of the key components of social studies instruction is teaching students to make informed decisions based on their situation. This activity will allow each student to assume the identity of an immigrant coming to the United States at the turn of the twentieth century. The students must make choices as to what items they will or will not bring on such a journey.

## Early Production

In addition to helping all students develop decision making skills and teaching them about hardships faced by immigrants coming to this country, this activity will also allow students to create pictures of everyday items and then practice saying their names.

## Materials

Personal possession of teacher, five empty boxes, blank and construction paper, markers, tape, scissors

## Strategy

1. Show one of your favorite possessions to the class. Ask the students to list some of their favorite possessions; compile a class list on the board.
2. Explain to the students that many of the people who came to the United States were only allowed to bring belongings that would fit in one steamer trunk or suitcase.
3. Divide students into five groups and hand out the empty boxes. Tell students they are to decorate their boxes as if they were steamer trunks (a photo or picture of a trunk or suitcase would be helpful in conveying the concept). The students can cut the lid off and tape it together and create a tape "hinge" so that it opens like an authentic trunk or suitcase.
4. Ask students to choose ten items that they would take with them on a trip to the United States. (Remember to have the students choose items that would have existed in the time period of 1880-1920; no video games or televisions, for example). Have them draw simple pictures of their chosen possessions on construction paper and label.
5. After each student has filled his or her trunk with drawings, pair students, making sure that any ELLs are matched with native speakers. Have students show their items and name them to their partner, then switch. Tell native speakers to say and write any names their partners don't know in English. Then, systematically go around the room and ask each student to name the items that he/she has chosen. By doing so, the students will not only practice saying the names of common items, but they can also observe what others have chosen and possibly learn new words.
6. The teacher will then debrief the students and find out what factors went into the decisions that were made regarding items to include in the journey by asking the following questions:
    - What is the most important item you decided to bring?
    - Did you remember to bring some food?
    - Did you remember to bring warm clothes?
    - What did you leave behind that you will miss the most?
    - Did you bring anything that you shouldn't have?

Note: Be sure to check the ELL students' comprehension of the questions; if there is any confusion, paraphrase the question, highlighting the main words on the board so they can look them up in bilingual dictionaries and/or use pictures.

Since the Bureau of the Census began keeping data on the foreign-born population in the U.S., it is clear that the United States has hosted families with many different home languages.[3] While contemporary immigration patterns are proportionally nowhere as large as the 26 million immigrants who came to the United States between 1880 and 1920, immigration is still an important historical concept that needs to be understood by current students in our classrooms. Although ELL students have a variety of experiences in how they came to the United States, they oftentimes share many of the hardships that other immigrants do. By examining the successes and failures of immigration throughout our nation's history, the students can learn that they are not alone in their quest to find their place in the American nation.

### Speech Emergence

This activity allows students to analyze and categorize various causes of immigration as either a *push* or a *pull* factor. It also allows the students to use maps to further develop geography skills.

### Materials

Blank political map of the world (these can be obtained online, e.g., http://geography.about.com/science/geography/cs/blankoutlinemaps/index.htm), Immigration Worksheet

### Strategy

1. Ask students, "Why do people move from one nation/country to another?" List student responses on the board. (The teacher may want to ask if anyone wants to share why he or she came to the United States. Do not make this mandatory so as to preserve privacy.)
2. Define the terms *push factors* and *pull factors* to the students. (Push factors are reasons that cause people to leave the place in which they are living; pull factors are reasons that cause people to come to a place to live from another place.)
3. Ask the students to look for any similarities between push and pull factors. Explain that reasons such as "better job" or "more freedom" can be described either as a push or a pull factor, depending on the perspective.
4. Distribute a blank political map of the world to students. Ask students to label the United States and any other countries with which they are familiar. After they have done this, help the students label the following countries: Bosnia, China, Cuba, England, Guatemala, Italy, Ireland, Mexico, and Russia.
5. Depending on the proficiency levels of your students, you can provide a brief explanation or lecture on the different reasons that people left the countries listed to come to the United States. Be sure to use visual supports such as overhead transparencies or the blackboard. As students listen to the reasons for the respective immigration patterns, they will fill in the blanks on the worksheet. Students should start to see that in most cases, economics plays a large role in the decision-making process that leads to people coming to the United States.
6. Put students in groups of four, number each group, and ask students to count off in the group. Draw a number between one and four and tell students to discuss the first question in each of the following sets of four questions. Make sure the person whose number was drawn can simply state the answer. If the student is an ELL student who needs extra support, the teammates can jointly write a simple response for the student to read/repeat. Then draw a number for a group and ask the selected member to respond. Continue this process with each question:
   1. What are some of the main reasons that people have come to live in the United States?
   2. Do you think more people come to or leave the United States every year?
   3. Is there another country you would prefer to live in rather than the U.S.? Why or why not?
   4. What do you think might be the hardest part of leaving one's native country and resettling in the U.S.?

**Immigration Worksheet**

| Country of Origin | "Push" Factor(s) | "Pull" Factor(s) |
|---|---|---|
| Bosnia | | |
| China | | |
| Cuba | | |
| England | | |
| Guatemala | | |
| Italy | | |
| Ireland | | |
| Mexico | | |
| Russia | | |

## Studying the Triangle Shirtwaist Company Fire

Historically, immigrants in the United States have faced many hardships due to their inability to speak English effectively. In the early twentieth century, many immigrants, especially women, had no alternative but to work in garment factories under very unsafe working conditions. This activity allows students to examine the consequences at one New York factory in which a fire broke out killing 146 women. By assuming the identities of different parties involved in the tragedy, the students will understand several prevailing viewpoints of this time period. This is based on a pedagogic strategy using a similar real-life scenario.[4] Ultimately, students will gain a greater understanding of why unions were later formed and why it was necessary for the United States government to mandate safer conditions for workers.

### Intermediate Fluency

By reading the account of the Triangle Shirtwaist Factory fire, the ELL student will strengthen reading comprehension and learn or review vocabulary such as strike and lock-out. By allowing the students to write responses based on what they have read, this activity reinforces collaborative learning, while also accessing the affective domain and encouraging students to consider the rights of workers and related government policies.

For more background on the fire and to see pictures of the Triangle Shirtwaist Factory, you can visit http://www.ilr.cornell.edu/trianglefire/photos on the World Wide Web. An excellent young adult book on the event is Michelle M. Houle's *Triangle Shirtwaist Factory Fire.* [5]

### Materials

Background Information Sheet on the Triangle Shirtwaist Fire; Identity Sheets, blank paper for students' responses

### Strategy:

1. Begin by asking the students to list several different types of jobs. Through probing and prompting, ensure that a wide range is included. Write these occupations on the board. Then ask the students to choose which of these jobs might be done by people who have limited command of English.
2. Explain to the students that in the early twentieth century, many immigrants that came to the United States from Europe didn't speak English and therefore had to take low-paying jobs in factories. Many women worked in the textile industry, sewing clothes for people to wear. In one such factory, the Triangle Shirtwaist Company, a fire broke out killing 146 people who were trapped inside.
3. Give students five minutes to silently read "Background Information on the Triangle Shirtwaist Factory Fire"(below), allowing ELL students to look up any words in the dictionary. The main words and terms are underlined in the student copy to facilitate comprehension. Pair students and ask them to restate the main points of the text in sixty seconds (each partner takes a turn restating). Another support strategy is to distribute readings to ELL students a day or two before so that they have time to get help with unknown vocabulary or structures. Note that the main words in the reading have been underlined to aid in comprehension.
4. Assign the students to one of four groups, and hand each group an Identity Sheet which it is to role-play.
5. After each group has read its Identity Sheet, allow sufficient time for them to respond in writing. Ask the groups to elect a spokesperson to read their response to the whole class.
6. Upon completion of each group's reading, ask the class the following questions:

a. Who do you think was to blame for the fire at the factory?

b. Was it right to ask workers to work in such unsafe conditions?

c. Are there any jobs today that are as dangerous as working in a shirt factory such as the one in the story?

d. Does the United States have any laws that protect workers in today's society? (You might want to briefly mention workers' compensation and OSHA, the Occupational Safety Health Administration.)

e. What do you think happened because of this fire?

7. Closure: Explain to the students that as a direct result of the Triangle Factory fire, people forced the passage of laws to improve working conditions in New York's factories. In 1912, a law was passed that made factory owners install sprinklers in buildings over seven stories with more than 200 people employed above the seventh floor. Also, fire alarms were installed in all buildings over two stories high, and in these buildings, fire drills were practiced once every three months. Finally, a new law ordered that all waste in factories be put in fireproof boxes and that no such waste be allowed to accumulate on the floor.

---

## Background Information on the Triangle Shirtwaist Fire

The Triangle Shirtwaist Company employed 500 women (mostly East European immigrants) and was located on the eighth, ninth, and tenth floors of the Ashe building in New York City. At approximately 4:30 p.m. on March 25, 1911, a fire broke out in the cutting room on the eighth floor. The cutting room floor was littered with extra pieces of cloth and the fire spread quickly. Most women on the eighth floor were able to escape to safety below, and most women on the tenth floor fled to the roof, where they survived the fire. The doors on the ninth floor, however, were locked to keep women from leaving their machines or from stealing cloth during the day. Historical records indicate that the ninth floor of the factory was overcrowded. The sewing machine tables were crammed so close together that there was little aisle space in which to move. Paper patterns and scraps of fabric were scattered everywhere and caught fire quickly.

The rear fire escape on the building collapsed and when the fire department arrived, their ladders would only reach to the sixth floor. To avoid burning to death, many women jumped from open windows. In less than fifteen minutes, 146 women were killed.

Less than two years earlier, workers in the Triangle Shirtwaist Factory had gone on strike to demand unlocked doors and sufficient fire escapes at their workplace. The management of the Triangle Shirtwaist Factory had responded by locking out its 500 strikers and by advertising for replacement workers. If the management had listened to the workers, the tragedy could have been avoided.

For more background on the fire and to see pictures of the Triangle Shirtwaist Factory, you can visit http://www.ilr.cornell.edu/trianglefire/photos on the World Wide Web.

### Sources

Hadley Davis, "Reform and the Triangle Shirtwaist Company Fire," *The Concord Review* (Fall 1988): 5-17. Retrieved August 30, 2002 from http://www.tcr.org/triangle.html.

Kenneth Jackson, ed. "Triangle Shirtwaist Fire" in *The Encyclopedia of New York City* (New Haven, CT: Yale University Press, 1995). Retrieved June 24, 2002 from http://www.yale.edu/yup/ENYC/triangle_shirtwaist.html.

Kheel Center for Labor-Management Documentation and Archives, "Triangle Factory Fire." Retrieved June 19, 2002 from http://www.ilr.cornell.edu/trianglefire/photos.

Identity # 1

# Rose Safran, Shirtwaist Factory Worker

You are Rose Safran, and you have worked at the Triangle Shirtwaist Factory for more than four years. Many of your best friends were lost in the fire, and you believe it is a tragedy that could have been avoided. If the management at the Triangle Factory had listened to you two years ago, they would have made the factory a safer place to work. You want to tell everyone about the terrible working conditions that your fellow shirt factory workers had to endure. The exits were blocked, the floor was littered with paper and cloth and the aisles were too small for many people to use at once. You think that Mr. Smith, the factory owner, should be punished for allowing the women to work in such unsafe conditions that ultimately caused their deaths.

Write a letter to the newspaper telling everyone how you feel about the fire.

**Identity # 2**

# Joseph Smith, Shirtwaist Factory Manager

You are Joseph Smith, and you own the Triangle Shirtwaist Factory. You feel very bad about how many women lost their lives, but it certainly isn't your fault. The doors of the factory needed to be locked to keep the women working and to keep the women from stealing cloth. When you tried unlocking the doors, women left early and many yards of cloth were missing. It is your job to see that the factory owner has the greatest amount of profit with the lowest possible costs. The more machines that you put in the factory, the more cloth you can prepare and the more money the factory can make. The government talks about making the owners improve conditions, but they don't offer us any money to help with the cost. If the owner had to spend thousands of dollars to improve the fire escapes and to install a sprinkler system, dozens of workers would have to be laid off to pay for it. Why isn't anyone blaming the fire department? They should have taller ladders to rescue people when a fire occurs. If the fire department had longer ladders, many of these women wouldn't have jumped to their deaths. Besides, Fire Marshall Beers said that there are more than 140 buildings in this city that are more dangerous than this. Also, these women came here even though they knew that it was dangerous, and although it is sad that many died, no one forced them to work.

Write a letter to the newspaper explaining your side of the story.

# Edward Worth, Fire Battalion Chief

You arrived on the scene just after the fire started. Unfortunately, the ladders on your fire trucks only reached to the sixth floor. Your hoses didn't reach all the way up to the eighth floor and you had to wait for other fire companies to arrive so that you could attach the hoses together. Your men tried to put out safety nets to catch the women who jumped from the building, but they were going too fast for the nets to stop their fall. What the building needed was a sprinkler system that would spray water on the fire to put it out before it spread. In your opinion, every building that is more than three stories high should have a sprinkler system in it so that tragedies such as these can be avoided. Also, the fire department should be allowed to inspect factory buildings to ensure that they are safe places to work. There are more than 140 factory buildings in New York right now that are far worse than the Triangle Shirtwaist building; hopefully this fire will open people's eyes, and something will be done.

Write a letter to the newspaper explaining what you think should be done.

Identity # 4

# Robert Wagner, Senator

As both a member of Congress and of the Commission on Fire Safety, you are appalled at the conditions at the Triangle Shirtwaist Factory. You want to pass strict new laws that will force factory owners to make their factories safer for workers. You think that all factory buildings taller than three stories should have to practice fire drills, they should have to install sprinklers and fire alarms, and that every floor should have a fire escape that is inspected yearly. You want to pass a law that makes it illegal to operate a factory if these conditions aren't met. If business owners can't afford to make their places of business safe, then they should be forced to close down. Workers should not have to come to work in a place that endangers their lives.

Write a letter to the newspaper about the new law that you want to pass.

## Notes

1. National Center for Education Statistics, *The Nation's Report Card: U.S. History Highlights 2001* (Washington, D.C.: National Center for Education Statistics [NCES], 2002).

2. Michael A. Fletcher, "Study: History Still a Mystery to Many Students," *Washington Post* (May 10, 2002): A3.

3. Campbell J. Gibson and Emily Lennon, *Historical Census Statistics on the Foreign-born Population of the United States: 1850-1990* (Washington, DC: U.S. Bureau of the Census, 1999): 3.

4. Bárbara C. Cruz, "Putting a Human Face on Natural Disasters: Using the 1985 Mexico City Earthquake as a Case Study," *Trends and Issues* 10, no. 4 (Winter 1998): 30-35.

5. Michelle M. Houle, *Triangle Shirtwaist Factory Fire* (Berkeley Heights, NJ: Enslow Publishers, 2002).

## Learned Societies and Useful History Websites

American Memory
http://lcweb2.loc.gov/amhome.html

American Originals
http://www.archives.gov/exhibit_hall/american_originals_iv/impact.html

The American Historical Association
http://www.theaha.org

The American Presidency
http://gi.grolier.com/presidents/preshome.html

Ben's Guide to U.S. Government for Kids
http://bensguide.gpo.gov

National Center for History in the Schools
http://www.sscnet.ucla.edu/nchs

National Council for History Education (NCHE)
http://www.history.org/nche

Organization of American Historians
http://www.indiana.edu/~oah

Organization of History Teachers
http://users.rcn.com/viceroy1/OHT.htm

Society for History Education (SHE), publisher of the quarterly journal *The History Teacher*
http://www.csulb.edu/~histeach

Who's Who in American History
http://us.history.wisc.edu/hist102/bios/bios.html

U.S. History Out Loud
http://www.hpol.org

# CHAPTER 6

# World History

World history—tracing human experience across the globe and through time—is a dreaded subject for many teachers because of the vast amount of content. Yet world history also provides many opportunities for innovative teaching and learning in line with the second theme of the social studies standards, ❶ TIME, CONTINUITY, AND CHANGE. World history teachers help students understand the world's rich and varied past, while simultaneously equipping them with strategies to understand our diverse nation and global society. Some scholars maintain that the study of the global human story is so central to the school curriculum that they advocate placing world history at its core.[1]

Seventy percent of U.S. public high schools offer world history courses.[2] However, many historians and educators lament that secondary teachers are often unprepared to teach the content, citing that few have direct college preparation in history.[3] Further, many world history textbooks have been charged with having a European bias, or, more specifically, a British-American bias. For example, some texts seem to minimize Spain's impact on Mesoamerica and the emergence of Latin America.[4] Others seemingly ignore important events in Asia and Africa in their account of world history.

Educators are, nevertheless, hopeful that the world history curriculum is changing for the better. A new "environmental perspective" is being touted as a more balanced approach to infusing more ecological views and social history into the teaching of world history.[5] The Advanced Placement exam started including questions reflecting this scholarly approach in 2001.

In terms of instructional strategies, this content area is rich with possibilities. The National Council for History Education encourages world history teachers to "go beyond the textbook," incorporate hands-on learning, and utilize authentic assessment strategies.[6] In addition to timelines, world history teachers can use graphic organizers, semantic mapping, and realia to explore ancient history as well as current international events. Hands-on projects (e.g., dioramas of ancient civilizations, construction of important sea vessels, and scenery for role-plays) provide kinesthetic learning opportunities and allow all students to contribute to the classroom community.

The activities that follow offer a wide range of teaching strategies that will help ELL students as well as provide all students with meaningful learning activities. Suggestions for all levels of language development (Preproduction, Early Production, Speech Emergence, and Intermediate Fluency) are provided. Three diverse topics in world history are presented here: the Columbian Encounter, the Industrial Revolution, and Hammurabi's Code. To set the stage and establish the diverse cultural and historical connections already present in the classroom, an introductory lesson, "World Origins of Our Class," is designed to underscore the students' global connections.

# World Origins of Our Class

One of the adages heard time and again is that the United States is a melting pot of the world's cultures. This activity examines students' global connections, fosters intergenerational communication, develops research skills, and can lead to positive self-esteem and appreciation for diversity. By incorporating students' personal stories and their cultural knowledge and experiences, the activity supports the understanding of social studies content.[7] It also incorporates an oral history approach, which can be beneficial in developing language skills, learning new concepts, and developing a link between the home and the school.[8]

## Preproduction
This activity allows students to gather data in their home languages and then apply it to a communal world map logged by all the students in the class. In a subsequent class discussion, yes/no questions asked in simplified language facilitate student participation.

## Materials
"Family Interviews" activity sheet; wall map of world; thumbtacks or push pins; yarn or string

## Strategy
1. Distribute the "Family Interviews" activity sheet and explain to students that they are to interview two older family members and gather the data asked for on the sheet. The family members need not be living with the student. The interview can be completed over the telephone as well as in person. Allow one school week for the collection of the data.
2. After conducting the interviews of their family members, students bring the data back to class. Make available one bulletin board or wall with a map of the world on it. Have students construct a composite map, noting with thumbtacks or push pins the country origins of students in the class. Using yarn or string, connect all the points on the map to the school's location.

## Questioning Strategy (can include, but not limited, to)
1. How many countries on our map have a pin?
2. What are the names of some countries on our map that have a pin?
3. What part of the world has the most number of pins?
4. Is there a region of the world that does not have a pin?
5. Which location is farthest from our school?
6. How many different languages are spoken in these countries?

## Extension Activity (Geography and Math Concepts)
You may want to use data collected during this activity to introduce and/or reinforce the bar graph (vertical/horizontal). Origins data can be categorized into world regions or continents (North America, Latin America, the Caribbean, Europe, Africa, Asia, etc.) and students can construct a bar graph showing the distribution of their relatives according to world region. If your students are already organized into small learning groups, each group may develop its own bar graph, and these may be combined into one graph showing the total distribution for the entire class.

**Family Interviews**

## Family Member #1: _____    Relation to You: _____

What is your date of birth?

Where were you born? (city, country)

Where were your parents born? (city, country)

Where were your grandparents born? (city, country)

What ethnic or cultural group do you feel you belong to the most?

Do you speak a language other than English? If yes, which one(s)?

Which special holidays, if any, do you observe? Describe how they are celebrated or commemorated?

Do you follow special traditions that come from other countries? If so, which?

NOTES:

## Family Member #2: _____    Relation to You: _____

What is your date of birth?

Where were you born? (city, country)

Where were your parents born? (city, country)

Where were your grandparents born? (city, country)

What ethnic or cultural group do you feel you belong to the most?

Do you speak a language other than English? If yes, which one(s)?

Which special holidays, if any, do you observe? Describe how they are celebrated or commemorated?

Do you follow special traditions that come from other countries? If so, which?

NOTES:

For many years, Columbus's historic 1492 voyage was characterized simply as a "discovery" of new lands. This insensitive and overly simplistic view ignored the peoples who already inhabited the Americas and all of their accomplishments. In addition to considering other perspectives when teaching about Columbus's voyages, the topic is especially fruitful in discussing the wide- and far-reaching consequences of contact between hemispheres. This lesson will underscore the importance of cultural diffusion while strengthening geographic skills. Teachers are encouraged to consult Alfred W. Crosby's influential 1973 work, *The Columbian Exchange*. The interchange included animal and plant exchanges, pathogens, human migrations (forced and voluntary), and the cultural exchanges of ideas, technology, and other human artifacts.

### Early Production
In this lesson, students consider the plant exchanges made possible by the Columbian encounter. Simple "who, what, where, and either/or" questions requiring one-word answers help support understanding.

### Teacher Background Preparation
See "Suggested Teacher Reading."

### Materials
One class set of blank world maps (this can be obtained online, e.g., http://geography.about.com/cs/blankoutlinemaps/index.htm?once=true&); transparency of "World Harvest"; "World Harvest" worksheet

### Strategy
1. Display "World Harvest" transparency. Explain and discuss.
2. Distribute "World Harvest" worksheet to students. Have students complete the activity sheets based on the information displayed on the transparency.
3. Distribute blank world maps. Have students apply directional arrows to their maps based on the information displayed on their worksheet.
4. Lead a class discussion using the questions at the bottom of the worksheet.

### Suggested Teacher Reading on the Columbian Encounter
Asimov, Issac. *Christopher Columbus: Navigator to the New World*. Wisconsin: Dareth Stevens Children's Books, 1991.

Axtell, James, Carla R. Phillips, and David J. Weber, eds. *Imagining the Other: First Encounters in North America*. Washington, D.C.: American Historical Association, 1991.

Clare, John. *The Voyages of Christopher Columbus*. NY: Gulliver Books, 1992.

Crosby, Alfred W. *The Columbian Exchange: Biological and Cultural Consequences*. Westport, CT: Greenwood Publishing Group, 1973.

Crosby, Alfred W. *The Columbian Voyages, the Columbian Exchange, and Their Historians*. Washington, D.C.: American Historical Association, 1987.

DeRubertis, Barbara. *Holidays and Heroes: Columbus Day*. New York: Kane Press, 1992.

Jacobs, Francine. *The Taínos: The People Who Welcomed Columbus*. New York: Putnam's Sons, 1992.

Krensky, Stephen. *Who Really Discovered America?* NY: Hastings House, 1987.

Kupperman, Karen Ordahl, David J. Weber, and Carla L. Phillips, eds. *North America and the Beginnings of European Colonization*. Washington, D.C.: American Historical Association, 1992.

Neal, Harry Edward. *Before Columbus: Who Discovered America?* NY: Julian Messner, 1981.

# A World Harvest

Using the information provided by your teacher, fill in the following chart.

| Foods Indigenous to the Americas | Introduced to Americas by Europeans |
|---|---|
| | |
| | |
| | |
| | |
| | |
| | |

1. Was it possible to make pizza (crust, tomato sauce, cheese) before the Columbian encounter?
2. Before Columbus's trip, who would have been able to make hot chocolate: an Aztec in ancient Mexico or an Englishman in London?
3. True or False: Bananas were first grown in the Caribbean.
4. Which of these foods do you eat most?
5. Did the origins of any of these foods surprise you?

# A World Harvest

| Indigenous to the Americas | Introduced to Americas by Europeans |
| --- | --- |
| potato | sugarcane |
| sweet potato | rice |
| corn | olives |
| squash | bananas |
| peanuts | barley |
| chile peppers | wheat |
| cotton | beets |
| cocoa | broccoli |
| tomato | carrots |
| avocado | lettuce |
| papaya | onions |
| pineapple | |

In addition to stressing critical thinking skills, the teaching of history should include an understanding of chronology and historical periods.[9] Timelines are useful in helping students to understand cause and effect and to develop insights into the consequences of people's actions and decisions. They provide a dramatic visual representation of how developments unfold.

### Speech Emergence

Students demonstrating Speech Emergence can speak in phrases and sentences and can engage in group discussions, provided there is teacher scaffolding. Therefore, the teacher will begin to incorporate "how" and "why" questions and place students in supportive, cooperative learning groups.

### Materials

"Inventions of the Industrial Revolution" worksheet and transparency master; overhead projector; assorted inventions (e.g., clothespin, light bulb, telephone, sticky note, and wristwatch.)

### Strategy

1. Display each of the inventions brought to class while stating the name for each. Ask students what the inventions all have in common. Probe and prompt so students conclude that they were all important inventions in their time.
2. Using one of the blank worksheets as a master, create and display "Inventions of the Industrial Revolution" (have answers available for your viewing nearby). Distribute worksheet to students.
3. Have students fill in their worksheets while you fill in the transparency master on the projector. As you fill in each of the boxes, explain the invention (using gestures and visuals), and direct students to fill in their own worksheets.
4. Lead a class discussion by asking the following questions, adding your own:
   a. Which invention is most important to you personally?
   b. Which invention do you think had the most impact on world history?
   c. Which do you think has created the most problems for humans? For the environment?
5. Closure: Ask students to guess about some inventions likely in the next 50-100 years.

### Extension Activity

Have students create a timeline using their worksheets.

Answer Key
## Inventions of the Industrial Revolution

| Name | Description | Year | Inventor |
|---|---|---|---|
| steam engine | provides energy for machines | 1765 | James Watt |
| cotton gin | separates seeds from cotton | 1793 | Eli Whitney |
| battery | first to store electricity | 1800 | Alessandro Volta |
| photographs | permanent images | 1834 | Fox Talbot |
| telegraph | long distance communication | 1836 | Samuel F.B. Morse |
| sewing machine | joins pieces of fabric or leather | 1844 | Elias Howe |
| dynamite | explosive | 1867 | Alfred Nobel |
| typewriter | writing machine | 1873 | Christopher Sholes |
| telephone | voice message transmission | 1876 | Alexander Graham Bell |
| phonograph | a.k.a. record player | 1877 | Thomas Edison |
| light bulb | produces light | 1879 | Thomas Edison |
| motion picture camera | moving pictures | 1892 | Thomas Edison |
| diesel engine | efficient petroleum engine | 1892 | Rudolf Diesel |
| x-rays | diagnostic tool | 1895 | Wilhelm Roentgen |
| wireless telegraph/radio | system of communication | 1895 | Guglielmo Marconi |
| moving assembly line | factory system | 1913 | Henry Ford |
| quartz clock | very accurate timekeeper | 1928 | W. A. Marrison |

# Inventions of the Industrial Revolution

| Name | Description | Year | Inventor |
|------|-------------|------|----------|
|      |             |      |          |
|      |             |      |          |
|      |             |      |          |
|      |             |      |          |
|      |             |      |          |
|      |             |      |          |
|      |             |      |          |
|      |             |      |          |
|      |             |      |          |
|      |             |      |          |
|      |             |      |          |
|      |             |      |          |
|      |             |      |          |
|      |             |      |          |
|      |             |      |          |
|      |             |      |          |

# Hammurabi's Code

Many students are surprised to learn that ancient Mesopotamian culture was quite sophisticated. Great strides were made in science and mathematics. Some of the most technologically advanced and beautiful buildings of the era were found in this society. Clay tokens were used for trade with other peoples; the development of the wheel and specialized sail boats facilitated trade. The development of writing was also enhanced with the advent of cuneiform ("word-pictures" carved onto clay tablets). The society is also known for one of the earliest law codes.

## Intermediate Fluency

Because learners at the Intermediate Fluency stage can engage in extended and more complex dialogue, they are able to participate in more complex problem solving and writing activities. In this activity, students will analyze Hammurabi's Code, compare it to contemporary laws, draft their own laws for their classroom, or draft a law on an issue important to them.

## Materials

Teacher Background Reading; class set of Hammurabi's Code (use a simplified version—either the version provided or one found on a number of websites, e.g., http://www.csd.k12.wi.us/HAMMURAB.HTM; http://www.eduplace.com/ss/hmss/6/unit/act3.1blm1.html; http://www.wsu.edu:8080/~wldciv/world_civ_reader/world_civ_reader_1/hammurabi.html)

## Strategy

1. Familiarize yourself with Hammurabi's Code by reading the Teacher Background Reading. Access Hammurabi's Code on the Internet or use the master provided. Photocopy a class set.
2. Distribute Hammurabi's Code to each student. Go over it as a class, highlighting a few laws, and explaining briefly.
3. Place students into groups of three. Ask students to either suggest laws for their classroom or brainstorm ideas for laws about an issue important to them.
4. Have small groups share their results with the rest of the class.

## Teacher Background Reading

Hammurabi was the King of Babylonia from 1792 to 1750 B.C. He is credited with uniting the many city-states under one religion and government. His reign is often referred to as "The Golden Age of Babylon." Advances made at that time in science, mathematics, and architecture are still evidenced today. For example, our systems of 360 degrees in a circle, 60 minutes in an hour, and 60 seconds in a minute are derived from the Babylonians' use of the sexagesimal number system (numbers having a base of 6). But Hammurabi's greatest claim to fame was the system of codified law that was hailed as a consistent, equitable way to handle disputes. These laws governed Babylonian life.

The code consists of 282 articles and is carved on an 8-foot-tall black stone column in 3,600 lines of cuneiform. In 1902, it was found at Souza, Iran by archaeologist Jacques de Morgan. It is currently on exhibit at the Louvre Museum in Paris. The code addresses a wide variety of economic and social issues, such as: business, labor, property rights, loans, family relations, and personal injuries. Hammurabi's code of laws provides the first record of the regulation of doctors' practices, as well as the regulation of their fees. A summary of the laws can be found at: http://www.csd.k12.wi.us/HAMMURAB.HTM.

The code was hailed as an instrument of justice, seeking to protect the poor and weaker members of society (including women, children, and slaves) against the unfair practices of the rich and powerful. In the case of criminal law, however, the code was harsh and retributive.

# SELECTED LAWS FROM
# HAMMURABI'S CODE

1   If a person accuses someone of a crime, but does not prove what he has charged, he shall, if it be a capital offense charged, be put to death.

2   If any one steals the property of a temple or of the court, he shall be put to death, and also the one who receives the stolen thing from him shall be put to death.

3   If any one steals the minor son of another, he shall be put to death.

4   If any one breaks a hole into a house (to steal), he shall be put to death before that hole and be buried.

5   If any one is committing a robbery and is caught, then he shall be put to death.

6   If fire breaks out in a house, and some one who comes to put it out cast his eye upon the property of the owner of the house, and takes the property of the master of the house, he shall be thrown into that self-same fire.

7   If any one opens his ditches to water his crop, but is careless, and the water floods the field of his neighbor, then he shall pay his neighbor corn for his loss.

8   If a son strikes his father, his hands shall be cut off.

9   If a man puts out the eye of another man, his eye shall be put out.

10  If he breaks another man's bone, his bone shall be broken.

## Notes

1. Simone Arias, Marilynn Hitchens, and Heidi Roupp, *Teaching World History: The Global Human Experience Through Time*. ERIC Digest April, 1998, ERIC Document Reproduction Service (ED 419 772).

2. Charlotte Crabtree and David O'Shea, *First Questions: A Preliminary Report on the Status of History in the Nation's Schools* (Los Angeles: National Center for History in the Schools, 1991), accessible on the Internet at http://www.woodrow.org/teachers/world-history/news/Charlotte.html.

3. Charlotte Crabtree and David O'Shea, "Teachers' Academic Preparation in History," *National Center for History in the Schools Newsletter* 1, no. 3 (November 1991): 4, 10.

4. William A. Paquette, "Putting the World into World History Textbooks," *Teaching History: A Journal of Methods* 26, no. 2 (Fall 2001): 71-89.

5. "History Gets a New World View," *NEA Today* 18, no. 7 (April 2000): 20. *NEA Today* is published by the National Education Association.

6. National Council for History Education, *Reinvigorating History in U.S. Schools: Recommendations for the States* (Washington, DC: NCHE Symposium, 1996). Accessed: May 7, 2002 at http://www.history.org/nche.

7. Joy Egbert and Carmen Simich-Dudgeon, "Providing Support for Non-Native Learners of English in the Social Studies Classroom," *The Social Studies* 92, no. 1 (2001): 22-25.

8. Irma Olmedo, "Creating Contexts for Studying History with Students Learning English," *The Social Studies* 87, no. 1 (Jan.-Feb. 1996): 39-44.

9. American Historical Association, *Criteria for Standards in History/Social Studies/Social Sciences*. Accessed: May 7, 2002 at http://www.theaha.org/teaching/standards.html

## Learned Societies and Useful World History Websites

Hyperhistory Online
http://www.hyperhistory.com/online_n2/History_n2/a.html

National Center for History in the Schools
http://www.sscnet.ucla.edu/nchs

National Council for History Education
http://www.history.org/nche

Society for History Education
http://www.csulb.edu/~histeach/#AboutSHE

Student's Friend – World History and Geography
http://www.studentsfriend.com/sf/sf.html

Teacher Explorer Center World History Lesson Plan Links
http://ss.uno.edu/ss/Links/WhLp.html

Teaching History
http://www.emporia.edu/socsci/journal/main.htm

Women in World History
http://www.womeninworldhistory.com/resources.html

World History Association (Woodrow Wilson Leadership Program for Teachers)
http://www.woodrow.org/teachers/world-history

The World History Association
http://www.thewha.org

World History Resources from Big Eye
http://www.bigeye.com/histworl.htm

# CHAPTER 7
# Geography

Geographic knowledge and skills are important for all social studies students. For the ELL student, however, the integral visual representations of geography (e.g., globes, maps, and charts) allow gains in proficiency in this subject area that are perhaps faster than in other areas that are more text dependent. With the help of these, students can develop "space and place" understanding, as well as more advanced concepts such as geographic perspective, relative location, and environmental interdependence.

According to National Council for the Social Studies, geographic study provides knowledge of Earth's physical and human systems while underscoring the interdependence of living things and physical environments. Studying geography arouses interest about the world and its diverse peoples and places. And because geography encompasses local, regional, and global issues, it allows students to understand and make decisions about issues at various levels.[1] Due to its all-encompassing nature, geography is relevant to all ten themes of the social studies standards developed by National Council for the Social Studies,[2] and is the specific focus of the third theme, ⦿ PEOPLE, PLACES, AND ENVIRONMENTS.

In 1994 the National Geography Standards, *Geography for Life*, were published. The geographically informed person is described as one who:

1. Sees meaning in the arrangement of things in space;
2. Understands relations between people, places, and environments;
3. Uses geographic skills; and
4. Applies spatial and ecological perspectives to life situations.

Six essential elements (spatial terms, places and regions, physical systems, human systems, environment and society, and the uses of geography) are further subdivided into eighteen standards.[3]

In 2001, the Nation's Report Card for Geography was issued.[4] It assessed students' geographic understanding at the fourth, eighth, and twelfth grades. The results were mixed. On the one hand, when results were compared to the 1994 test, fourth and eighth graders scored higher (although there was no difference among twelfth graders). However, the 2001 geography assessment showed that only 21 percent of fourth graders, 30 percent of eighth graders, and 25 percent of twelfth graders performed at or above the "proficient" level for their respective grades. Dismally, many newspapers reported one of the more alarming findings: that a third of fourth graders could not identify their own state on a U.S. map.[5] Educators responded that the results merely underscored what they had been saying all along—that this is one content area that needs considerable strengthening.

Since many ELL students or their parents may have come to the United States from another country, they may have firsthand knowledge of diverse geographic features not present in the U.S. This knowledge and experience can be helpful when studying other world regions and in comparing and contrasting the United States with other locations.

The remainder of this chapter includes activities that will allow students to identify simple, as well as complex, geographic features and will also offer the students the opportunity to create representations of the environment in which they live.

Creating dioramas has been shown to be an effective tool for meeting the challenge of teaching social studies to ELL students.[6] By first identifying and then creating replicas of physical features, the student can internalize the concepts easily. This activity provides students with the opportunity to create their own biosphere that contains several important geographic features. Although all students will be engaged learners, ELL students will particularly benefit from the concrete nature of the learning experience; learners who prefer kinesthetic activities will appreciate the hands-on project.

### Preproduction and Early Production
This activity will involve students watching the teacher identify several geographic features. The students will then create a diorama containing examples of these features.

### Materials
Pictures of mountains, rivers, lakes, hills, forests, deserts, and other common geographic regions, tape, shoe boxes, scissors, markers, crayons, or coloring pencils.

### Strategy
1. The teacher will begin by showing the students pictures of distinctly different geographic features and then having the students chorally repeat the respective names of each. Tape the pictures on the board and label them.
2. After the students have identified the different land and water formations, the students will be asked to create a model containing several of these features.
3. Students can draw and label different landforms and cut them out.
4. After the students have created the landforms, they will be asked to glue them into the shoe box, creating a three dimensional model of the different forms.
5. The teacher should list several features that must be included in all dioramas, as well as optional features that the students may include. Examples of optional features could be depictions of animals that live in the different areas or additional humanly constructed features that one might find in a given area (i.e., docks on shores, livestock on grassy plains, etc.).
6. After students have created their dioramas, they can share them with the class through a "walking gallery." Half the students stand by their displays while the other half visits each display and listens to the creator's description. By having students label each feature, the students can hear the pronunciation of each word. ELL students at pre-production level can listen and acquire new vocabulary.

### Questions
1. Which of these things do you find where you live? (Ask ELL students to point, using gestures and paraphrasing to explain question.)
2. Which do you like the most—a river, a lake, or the beach? Why? (Use pictures to indicate each type.)
3. In _____ (e.g., Laos or Mexico) are there _____ (Name the geographic feature and point to picture)?

# Scaling it Down: Creating a Model of Your Classroom

Since an integral part of understanding any map is understanding that the map is a replica of what is being portrayed, the students will investigate the concept of scale and create a map of their classroom that is drawn to scale.

## Early Production
The teacher will explain the concept of scale to students, and the students will have the opportunity to measure the dimensions of their classroom and create an overhead view of what their classroom looks like.

## Materials
Several maps (each using a different scale), drawing paper, pencils, rulers, tape measures to measure the dimensions of both the classroom and the items in the classroom

## Strategy
The teacher will begin by asking the students: *What is a map? Why do we use maps? How are they helpful?*
1. The teacher will then show several examples of maps and show that different maps are drawn at different scales. Explain the concept of scale. Use modeling and concrete examples, paraphrasing and restating.
2. The teacher will instruct the class that each student will be creating an overhead map of the classroom. The teacher will also tell the class that on their respective maps, the scale will be ½ inch = 1 foot. The teacher draws an example on the board.
3. The teacher will then ask students to use rulers or tape measures to measure the dimensions of the outer walls of the room, the dimensions of the desks, and any other piece of furniture that is in the room. Remind students that they also need to measure how far items are from the walls so that they can place them in the correct relative location on their maps.
4. Using a piece of paper, the students will then begin to draw an overhead view of the classroom. To make the exercise more concrete, the teacher can suggest cutting out models of desks and filing cabinets, so that the students can move them around to their appropriate places on the paper. Encourage students to create a map key that labels each item so that they may be understood by others.
5. After the students have created their map of the classroom, display the maps and compare the students' representations to the actual layout of the classroom.

## Questions
1. Why do we use maps? How are they helpful? (ELL students at this level might have a hard time answering but could listen.)
2. Which maps most closely represent how the classroom actually looks?
3. What are some of the mistakes that people made when creating their maps? (Write answers on board.) Do you think cartographers (map makers) make similar mistakes?
4. Why is it useful to draw everything on a map using the same scale? What would happen if we changed scale during the creation of our maps?

## Extension Activity
Show the students a political and a physical map of the United States. Ask the students how the maps are different. Ask the students why some maps show things that other maps do not. Explain to the students that no map shows everything and that while maps are useful in understanding the world, some information is always lost when looking at maps. Ask: Can you think of other types of maps—a map that shows neither the political nor the physical?

# Global Interdependence

Common objects that are found in our classrooms and in students' homes oftentimes come from faraway places. With the development of new technologies in communication and transportation, our world is quickly becoming a much smaller place. By examining where commonplace objects were created or assembled, students can come to the realization that we are truly part of a global community and that decisions made around the world can affect our everyday lives.

## Speech Emergence
In this activity, the students will examine objects found in the classroom as well as articles of clothing to identify the place from which they came. The students will list these countries and then find them on a map to compare and describe the distances the items have traveled as well as the location (both relative and absolute) from which these items originated.

## Materials
International Trade Worksheet, items from classroom, map of the world

## Strategy
1. First, the teacher will ask the students to identify some of the items found in their homes that they would not like to live without. The teacher will ask the students where they think most of these items were made.
2. The teacher will then ask the students to find a label on their clothes or an item in the classroom that identifies where it was made or assembled.
3. The teacher will list student responses on the board, and ask if anyone is surprised at the number of different countries from which these items have come.
4. The teacher will pass out the International Trade Worksheet and tell the students to work in pairs to complete the worksheet with items found in the classroom (e.g., pencils, calculators, chairs, desks, and clothes)
5. After the small groups have completed this worksheet, the teacher will have one person from each group come to a wall map of the world, or a world map handout, to place a piece of tape or a sticky note with the name of the item on the country from which the item originated.
6. After all of the groups have filled in an item, ask the students to look at the world map.
7. The teacher will ask the students questions based on their observations of the countries of origin for the various items.

## Questions
1. What country/countries produced the most goods used here in the U.S. by our class? Does this surprise you? Why?
2. Why do you think the U.S. receives so many goods from other countries?
3. Are most of the countries marked in this sample near or far away?
4. Where did most of the clothing items come from?
5. What methods do you think were used to transport these goods to the U.S.?

# International Trade Worksheet

| Item | Company | Country |
|------|---------|---------|
|      |         |         |
|      |         |         |
|      |         |         |
|      |         |         |
|      |         |         |
|      |         |         |
|      |         |         |
|      |         |         |
|      |         |         |
|      |         |         |

How many of these countries are in the Western Hemisphere? _____

How many of these countries are in the Eastern Hemisphere? _____

How many are countries whose locations you did not know? _____

Which ones? _____

**Notes**

1. National Council for the Social Studies, *Expectations of Excellence: Curriculum Standards for Social Studies* (Washington, D.C.: National Council for the Social Studies, 1994).

2. Cynthia Sunal and Mary Haas, *Social Studies for the Elementary and Middle Grades: A Constructivist Approach* (Boston, MA: Allyn & Bacon, 2002).

3. National Geographic Society, *Geography for Life: National Geography Standards* (Washington, DC: National Geographic Society, 1994).

4. Andrew R. Weiss, Anthony D. Lutkus, Barbara S. Hildebrant, and Matthew S. Johnson, *The Nation's Report Card: Geography 2001* (Washington, D.C.: U.S. Department of Education, 2002).

5. Michael Fletcher, "In Test, Students Lack Geography Knowledge," *Washington Post* (June 22, 2002): A9.

6. Deborah J. Short, "The Challenge of Social Studies for Limited English Proficient Students," *Social Education* 58, no. 1 (January 1994): 36-39.

## Learned Societies and Useful Geography Websites

Association of American Geographers
http://www.aag.org

American Geographical Society
http://www.amergeog.org

Blank Outline Maps of the World, Continents, Countries, and the U.S
http://geography.about.com/science/geography/cs/blankoutlinemaps/index.htm

Discovery School: Geography Lesson Plans
http://school.discovery.com/lessonplans/geog.html

Geographic Learning Site
http://geography.state.gov/htmls/statehome.html

Geography Action!
http://www.nationalgeographic.com/geographyaction

National Council for Geographic Education
http://www.ncge.org

National Geographic
http://www.nationalgeographic.com

National Geographic Maps and Geography
http://www.nationalgeographic.com/maps/index.html

Proteacher
http://www.proteacher.com/090027.shtml

Xpeditions
http://www.nationalgeographic.com/xpeditions

# CHAPTER 8

# Government and Civics

Long considered a cornerstone of social studies education, citizenship education helps students gain a greater understanding of the U.S. political system, the purpose, structure, and functions of government, and students' rights and responsibilities as citizens.[1] NCSS Standard **Ⓥ POWER, AUTHORITY, AND GOVERNANCE** focuses on this important social studies content area.

The origins of citizenship education in the U.S. in its present form date to the turn of the twentieth century, and were part of an effort to "Americanize" the diverse groups of immigrants arriving in large numbers. These programs, which were often referred to as "pressure cooker" civic education, persisted until the 1960s.[2] The civil rights era, with its attendant discord and disenchantment, led the way toward a more analytical, reflective, and comprehensive civics curriculum.

Although every state's curriculum guidelines note the need for civic education, "this important part of the student's overall education is seldom given sustained and systematic attention in the kindergarten through twelfth grade."[3] This is unfortunate because government and civics provide an ideal context for ELL students to develop language skills while learning about the political structure of their host country. Strategies such as graphic organizers, political cartoons, and visual dictionaries can simplify abstract concepts into understandable components.

We define good citizenship as participating knowledgeably in community affairs. The civic nature of the United States calls for full participation in a democratic society. This in turn entails an informed public, thoughtful voting, and monitoring of government activity and world events.

The good news is that, in general, U.S. students seem to score well on assessments centered on civic knowledge and skills. In 1999, the IEA Civic Education Study was conducted in twenty-eight countries. The study assessed the civic knowledge and skills of 14-year-olds and their attitudes toward democracy and citizenship. U.S. ninth-graders scored significantly above the international average on the total civic knowledge scale, and in no other country did students significantly outperform U.S. students.[4]

In 1999, the National Assessment of Educational Progress published the results of the 1998 civics assessment which evaluated the educational progress of students' civic knowledge at grades 4, 8, and 12. The majority of students performed at or above the "basic" level of civics achievement (69 percent, 70 percent, and 65 percent respectively for grades 4, 8, and 12). However, only 2 percent of the students at grades 4 and 8, and 4 percent at grade 12 performed at the highest achievement level, "advanced." Hispanic students scored significantly lower than other ethnic groups at all grade levels.[5] Clearly, there is still work to be done in this important content area.

In this chapter, the first unit of study focuses on the need for laws and how they are made in the U.S. Units 2 and 3 in this chapter are more global in scope and focus on international women's suffrage and on the issue of immigration. Although both topics have a long history in our nation, they are also timely and relevant and will continue to be so in the foreseeable future.

# Why Do We Need Laws? How Are They Made?

## Speech Emergence

Your ELL students will likely come from countries with a variety of legal and governmental systems. Students need to understand that every country has its own set of unique laws that reflect that country's history, culture, and, sometimes, principal religion. In the United States, laws are made by state and local governments as well as at the national level. In this lesson, students will consider why laws are necessary and learn how laws are made in the U.S. The lesson could also use graphics and diagrams recommended for the organization of information and as a means to explain key concepts and their relationships.[6]

## Materials

"How Laws Are Made" (class set)

## Strategy

1. Explain that national laws are those laws that everyone in the country must follow. Laws made by an individual state only apply in that state. Today the class will talk about how a law gets made at the national level. Ask students to provide examples of federal law (ELL students may not volunteer examples; be sure to write down responses on board to help facilitate understanding, using pictorial representations as well as words).
2. Distribute "How Laws Are Made," allowing ELL students to have access to their bilingual dictionaries. Read and explain each step, stopping to ask recall- and comprehension-level questions and to clarify specific points.
3. Give an example of a federal law. Ask the students to get in groups of four and round robin, each taking a turn to express why they think the law was enacted. Do the students agree with the law?

## Extension Activity

Have students draft a bill on an issue they consider important.

# How Laws Are Made

Laws may be initiated in either chamber of Congress, the House of Representatives or the Senate. For this example, we will track a bill introduced in the House of Representatives.

**1** When a Representative has an idea for a new law, s/he becomes the sponsor of that bill and introduces it by giving it to the clerk of the House or by placing it in a box, called the **hopper**. The clerk assigns a legislative number to the bill, with H.R. for bills introduced in the House and S. for bills introduced in the Senate. The Government Printing Office (GPO) then prints the bill and distributes copies to each representative.

**2** Next, the bill is assigned to a committee (the House has twenty-two standing committees, each with jurisdiction over bills in certain areas) by the Speaker of the House so that it can be studied.

The standing committee (or often a subcommittee) studies the bill and hears testimony from experts and people interested in the bill. The committee then may release the bill with a recommendation to pass it, or revise the bill and release it, or lay it aside so that the House cannot vote on it. Releasing the bill is called reporting it out, while laying it aside is called **tabling**.

**3** If the bill is released, it then goes on a **calendar** (a list of bills awaiting action). Here the House Rules Committee may call for the bill to be voted on quickly, limit the debate, or limit or prohibit amendments. Undisputed bills may be passed by unanimous consent, or by a two-thirds vote if members agree to suspend the rules.

**4** The bill now goes to the floor of the House for consideration and begins with a complete reading of the bill (sometimes this is the only complete reading). A third reading (title only) occurs after any amendments have been added. If the bill passes by simple majority (218 of 435), the bill moves to the Senate.

**5** In order to be introduced in the Senate, a senator must be recognized as the presiding officer and announce the introduction of the bill. Sometimes, when a bill has passed in one house, it becomes known as an **act**; however, this term usually means a bill that has been passed by both houses and becomes law.

**6** Just as in the House, the bill then is assigned to a committee. It is assigned to one of the Senate's sixteen standing committees by the presiding officer. The Senate committee studies and either releases or tables the bill just like the House standing committee.

**7** Once released, the bill goes to the Senate floor for consideration. Bills are voted on in the Senate based on the order they come from the committee; however, an urgent bill may be pushed ahead by leaders of the majority party. When the Senate considers the bill, they can vote on it indefinitely. When there is no more debate, the bill is voted on. A simple majority (51 of 100) passes the bill.

**8** The bill now moves onto a conference committee, which is made up of members from each House. The committee works out any differences between the House and Senate versions of the bill. The revised bill is sent back to both houses for their final approval. Once approved, the bill is printed by the Government Printing Office (GPO) in a process called **enrolling**. The clerk from the introducing house certifies the final version.

**9** The enrolled bill is now signed by the Speaker of the House and then the vice president. Finally, it is sent for presidential consideration. The president has ten days to sign or **veto** the enrolled bill. If the president vetoes the bill, it can still become a law if two-thirds of the Senate and two-thirds of the House then vote in favor of the bill.

Source: http://bensguide.gpo.gov/6-8/lawmaking/index.html

The right to vote is a significant component in exercising political power and effecting change. Suffrage is an important measure of full citizenship and often leads the way to obtaining other rights.[7] Historically, most countries have granted women suffrage at a later date than men and after much resistance. In some countries, the struggle continues, and thus women are not fully enfranchised worldwide.

### Speech Emergence

This lesson is intended to heighten awareness of women's suffrage, while also improving map skills, developing inferences about the processes that shape distribution patterns, and strengthening English language skills by encouraging collaborative discussion with peers. The latter has been shown to support ELL students' comprehension of social studies concepts.[8]

### Materials

"Pizza Ballot"; "Women's Vote Worldwide"; "Women's Suffrage"

### Strategy

1. As students come into the room, hand a "Pizza Ballot" to each female student. If asked about its meaning, say only that it will be explained as soon as class begins.
2. After students are all seated, ask them to pretend that they are planning a pizza party. The toppings will be of their choosing; however, only some students will have the right to vote for the toppings.
   Allow the voting to occur. (Of course, only the girls will have the opportunity to vote.) Collect all the ballots.
3. Discuss the experience by asking the following questions and writing the answers on the board:
   a. To ELL students: Who had the power—the females (women) or the males (men)?
   b. To males: How did you feel not having a voice in the decision making?
   c. To females: How did it feel to have all of the power?
   d. To males: Did any of you try to tell the females sitting close to you what to choose?
   e. To females: Did the males make you feel pressured when you were choosing? If yes, how did they influence you?
   f. To females: Did any of you feel bad about having all the power? Did any of you try to make fair choices for everyone in the room?
4. Distribute "Women's Vote Worldwide" to each student. Allow students to review the data.
5. Facilitate small group discussions by putting students in pairs and giving them the handout, "Women's Suffrage," with discussion questions, some of which require further research.

# Pizza Ballot

Which of the following toppings would you like on the pizza that we order for our pizza party?
Check all those that apply.

| | |
|---|---|
| Mushrooms | Onions |
| Peppers | Pineapple |
| Sausage | Pepperoni |
| Extra Cheese | Other |

# Women's Suffrage

In pairs, discuss and answer the following questions.

1.  Which countries granted suffrage before 1920? And before 1945?

2.  Which countries granted suffrage to women after 1945?

3.  Were there any countries that surprised you by their early granting of suffrage?

4.  Were there any countries that surprised you by their late granting of suffrage?

5.  Why do you think New Zealand and Australia were the first countries to grant women the right to vote?

6.  Why was the year 1917 significant for Russia? What happened in 1917 in Russia?

7.  What international event might have had an impact on women's suffrage in 1945? What happened in 1945?

8.  How does the United States compare to other countries in the world?

9.  Which decades had the greatest number of countries granting women suffrage? Why might that be? (Be sure to point out the many decolonization movements in the late 1950s.)

10. Which countries do not allow women to vote now?

# Women's Vote Worldwide

The following is a summary of selected countries that have granted women suffrage (the right to vote) and the dates of when that took place. There are still some countries where women cannot vote or have severe restrictions.

| YEAR | COUNTRIES |
|------|-----------|
| 1893 | New Zealand |
| 1902 | Australia |
| 1906 | Finland |
| 1913 | Norway |
| 1915 | Denmark, Iceland |
| 1917 | USSR |
| 1918 | Austria, Canada, Poland |
| 1919 | Czechoslovakia, Germany, Ireland, Luxembourg, Sweden, Netherlands |
| 1920 | United States |
| 1924 | Mongolia |
| 1928 | United Kingdom |
| 1929 | Ecuador |
| 1931 | Spain, Sri Lanka |
| 1932 | Brazil, Thailand, Uruguay |
| 1934 | Cuba, Turkey |
| 1935 | Burma |
| 1937 | Philippines |
| 1942 | Dominican Republic |
| 1944 | Bulgaria, Jamaica |
| 1945 | France, Guatemala, Hungary, Indonesia, Japan, Panama, Trinidad and Tobago |
| 1946 | Cameroon, Italy, Liberia, North Korea, Romania, Yugoslavia |
| 1947 | Argentina, Malta, Pakistan, Venezuela, Vietnam |
| 1948 | Belgium, Israel, South Korea |
| 1949 | Chile, China, Costa Rica, India |
| 1950 | Barbados, El Salvador |
| 1951 | Nepal |
| 1952 | Bolivia, Greece, Lebanon |
| 1953 | Mexico, Syria |
| 1954 | Colombia |
| 1955 | Ethiopia, Ghana, Nicaragua, Peru |
| 1956 | Egypt, Gabon, Ivory Coast, Mali, Mauritius, Senegal |
| 1957 | Honduras, Malaysia |
| 1959 | Cyprus, Madagascar, Morocco, Tanzania, Tunisia |

*Continued*

| YEAR | COUNTRIES |
|------|-----------|
| 1960 | Nigeria |
| 1961 | Burundi, Gambia, Paraguay, Rwanda, Sierra Leone |
| 1962 | Algeria, Uganda |
| 1963 | Iran, Kenya |
| 1964 | Malawi |
| 1965 | Afghanistan, Botswana |
| 1967 | Zaire |
| 1968 | Swaziland |
| 1969 | Libya |
| 1970 | Yemen Arab Republic |
| 1971 | Switzerland |
| 1974 | Jordan |
| 1976 | Portugal |
| 1980 | Iraq |
| 1981 | Liechtenstein |
| 1986 | Central African Republic |
| 1987 | Namibia |
| 1994 | South Africa |

Sources: International Women's Democracy Center (www.iwdc.org); United Nations Educational, Scientific and Cultural Organization (www.unesco.org/education/educprog/50y/brochure/tle/150.htm); Grolier Multimedia Encyclopedia, "Women's Suffrage," at http://gi.grolier.com/presidents/aae/side/wsffrg.html; the Women in World History Curriculum at http://www.womeninworldhistory.com/factLesson4.html; Ruth Leger Sivard, *Women...A World Survey*. Washington, D.C.: World Priorities, 1995. The dates given by the sources can differ because women's suffrage was granted in stages in a number of countries: for example, women first received the vote in the United Kingdom in 1918, when women aged 30 and over were allowed to vote, but at that time the age at which men could vote was 21, and women aged 21 or more were only granted the vote in 1928. Thus, the date 1928 is listed in this Table as the year of women's suffrage in the United Kingdom.

## Teacher Resources

The Encyclopedia Britannica Guide to Women's History
http://women.eb.com

Living the Legacy: The Women's Rights Movement
http://www.legacy98.org

The National Museum of Women's History
http://www.nmwh.org/exhibits/exhibit_frames.html

National Women's History Project
http://www.nwhp.org

Not For Ourselves Alone: Women's Suffrage
http://www.pbs.org/stantonanthony/wherearewe/index.html

One Woman, One Vote: The American Experience
http://www.pbs.org/onewoman/one_woman.html

Seager, Joni and Ann Olson. *Women in the World Atlas*. New York: Simon and Schuster, 1986.

Susan B. Anthony House
http://www.susanbanthonyhouse.org

Upstate New York and the Women's Rights Movement
http://www.lib.rochester.edu/rbk/women/women.htm

Woman Suffrage and the 19th Amendment
http://www.nara.gov/education/teaching/woman/home.html

# Whom Should We Allow In?

### Intermediate Fluency

One of the thorniest dilemmas facing our nation concerns immigration to the United States. This exercise allows students to consider whether some people should be given preference over others as immigrants to the United States. Acting as a facilitator, the teacher must be prepared for spirited student discussion and to work through some potentially prejudiced viewpoints. Because of the inherently controversial nature of the topic, the classroom teacher should use his or her professional judgement as to whether the activity is a suitable one for his or her class. Despite these caveats, this exercise underscores the difficulties of choice that confront us, especially when those choices concern our fellow human beings.

### Materials
Student resource sheet ("Whom Should We Allow In?")

### Strategy
1. Place students in groups of three or four. Explain that they are a panel of U.S. immigration officials who will be reviewing the backgrounds and credentials of ten people trying to gain entry into the United States. Because immigration is restricted to certain quotas per year, only four of the applicants can be allowed in.
2. Distribute "Whom Should We Allow In?" to each student allowing ELL students to have access to their bilingual dictionaries. Direct students to silently read through the cases first and, individually, rank them from most desirable (1) to least desirable (10) as U.S. citizens. After everyone has ranked the applicants as individuals, each group is to discuss its rankings, consider which characteristics should be most sought in immigrants, and decide which four applicants will be allowed entry into the U.S.
   [Alternate Strategy: You may also want to first present the scenarios with visuals and gestures and then group students to rank them.]
3. Ask each group to write its list of four (in rank order) on the board.
4. As a class, discuss the rankings and the discussions that led to their final decisions. Ask: Whom did you pick first—why?
5. Bring closure to the lesson by leading a discussion using the following questions:
   a. What is the most important thing to help you decide who can come to the United States?
   b. Should political immigrants be given priority over those who immigrate for economic reasons? [Explain, if necessary: a political immigrant is someone who comes to live in the U.S. because his or her political beliefs are not the same as the government's political beliefs in his or her country. An economic immigrant comes to live in the U.S. to find better job prospects.]
   c. Would your rankings be different if you could place certain conditions on the applicants (e.g., ineligibility for public assistance or learning English)?
   d. What might happen if the United States decided to stop all immigration into the country?
   e. Do you think the United States will ever need to stop immigration entirely? Why or why not?

# Whom Should We Allow In?

**Ricardo Flores:**
1. 34-year-old farmer from small town in Mexico where there is guerrilla violence
2. has a family (wife, mother, and four children) who will come with him
3. skilled agricultural worker who is willing to accept any work available; wife and mother also willing and able to work
4. speaks only Spanish.

**Chandra Patel:**
1. 42-year-old physician from India
2. he and his family (wife and three children) want a new start in the U.S.
3. Dr. Patel is internationally well-known as a cardiologist
4. will move to Atlanta where his uncle and two cousins live.

**Michael Collins:**
1. 29-year-old computer programmer from Ireland
2. has a high level of education and experience in computer science
3. has no family or friends in the U.S.
4. is HIV-positive.

**Francine Bouvier:**
1. 21-year-old fashion model from France
2. well-known in the U.S.; has been on the cover of several magazines
3. she wants to become an American citizen eventually
4. speaks little English but is starting a language course soon.

**Lydia Martínez:**
1. 65-year-old retired school teacher from Cuba
2. is sick and cannot get necessary medicines and treatment in her native country
3. she has two children in Miami who are willing to give her a home
4. speaks only Spanish.

**Li Chang:**
1. 25-year-old factory worker from China
2. he and his wife have one child but would like to have more (the "one-child policy" in China makes it difficult for them to have another child)
3. would like to settle in San Francisco where there is a large Asian community.

**Sonya Petrov:**
1. 14-year-old gymnast from Russia
2. she and her parents would like to move to the U.S. to increase Sonya's career prospects; they have hopes of her joining the American Olympic team
3. all three are fluent in English.

**François Pamphile:**
1. 50-year-old taxi driver from Haiti
2. single, no family
3. cannot make a living in Port-au-Prince because of his country's political and economic problems
4. speaks French, Creole, and some English.

**Hans Deutch:**
1. 34-year-old German with a petty criminal record
2. has been studying English for the past year
3. is willing to work at any job available although he has training as a diesel mechanic.

**Notes**

1. C. Frederick Risinger, "Citizenship Education and the World Wide Web," *Social Education* 61, no. 4 (1997): 223-224.

2. Mark C. Alexander, "Law-Related Education: Hope for Today's Students," *Ohio Northern University Law Review* 20, no. 1 (1993): 57-97.

3. Charles N. Quigley, "Civic Education: Recent History, Current Status, and the Future," *Albany Law Review* 62, no. 4 (1999): 1425.

4. Stephanie Baldi, Marianne Perie, Dan Skidmore, Elizabeth Greenberg, and Carole Hahn, *What Democracy Means to Ninth-Graders: U.S. Results From the International IEA Civic Education Study* (Washington, D.C.: U.S. Department of Education, 2001).

5. NAEP, *1998 Civics Report Card for the Nation* (published in 1999; date accessed: August 15, 2002).

6. Steve Moline, *I See What You Mean: Children at Work with Visual Information* (York, ME: Stenhouse, 1995).

7. Joni Seager, *State of the Women of the World Atlas* (New York: Penguin, 1997).

8. Carmen Simich-Dudgeon, "Classroom Strategies for Encouraging Collaborative Discussion," *Directions in Language and Education* 12 (Washington, D.C.: NCBE, 1998).

---

## Learned Societies and Useful Government & Civics Websites

Ben's Guide to U.S. Government for Kids
http://bensguide.gpo.gov

Center for Civic Education
http://www.civiced.org/index.html

Civic Mind
http://www.civicmind.com

Civic Practices Network
http://www.cpn.org/index.html

Civnet
http://civnet.org

Core Documents of U.S. Democracy
http://www.access.gpo.gov/su_docs/dpos/coredocs.html

Electronic Policy Network
http://epn.org

Internet Resources for Civic Educators
http://www.ed.gov/databases/ERIC_Digests/ed415176.html

Learning Adventures in Citizenship
http://www.thirteen.org/newyork/laic/index.html

National Archives and Records Administration
http://www.nara.gov/

Thomas: U.S. Congress on the Internet
http://thomas.loc.gov

U.S. Dept of State
http://www.state.gov

U.S. Dept of Justice
http://www.usdoj.gov/kidspage

The White House
http://www.whitehouse.gov

# CHAPTER 9

# Economics

It is imperative that all our students attain basic economic literacy and learn real-life skills that will allow them effectively to participate in the global economy (NCSS Standard ⑦ **PRODUCTION, DISTRIBUTION, AND CONSUMPTION**). According to the National Council on Economic Education, only 48 percent of American high school students have an adequate understanding of basic economic principles.[1] The fundamentals of money, credit, saving, and investing are critical for young people in at least two ways: first, because they participate in the economy; and second, because if they do not understand economic basics when they're young, as adults they are more likely to have money problems, career problems, and credit problems.

As educators, we may have even more of a responsibility to ELL students to promote their economic literacy. Since many of them are newly arrived immigrants, they may be totally unfamiliar with the U.S. economic system. Yet these students and their families are often participating members of the economy before they are fluent in English. Often, it is the ELL student who serves as cultural bridge between the home and society at large.

Some ELL students may come from economic systems very different from that found in the United States. European students may question U.S. trading policies. Students who emigrated from socialist systems may be overwhelmed by the number of product brands and persuasive advertising campaigns in the U.S. Students from emerging democracies may wonder about income and resource distribution.

The study of economics is heavily dependent upon language, both oral and written. Fortunately, because charts, graphs, and other visuals are often used in economic education, ELL students and their teachers will find these support structures helpful in understanding and explaining complex concepts and ideas. This content area also provides an opportunity to develop consumer and life skills so that all students are better prepared to participate in economic decision-making upon graduation.

The wide range of teaching strategies suggested below will help ELL students, and, indeed, provide all students with meaningful learning activities. Suggestions for all levels of language development (Preproduction, Early Production, Speech Emergence, and Intermediate Fluency) are provided. Four staple units in economic education—advertising, entrepreneurship, budgeting, and international trade—are explored.

## Advertising: Analysis of Marketing and Methods

The role advertising plays in our economic system has long been a unit of study in economic education. Since 1841 (when the first American advertising agency was opened in Philadelphia), advertising has been a mainstay of the U.S. economy and society.

Students are exposed to commercials from a variety of sources—at home, at the movies, on the Internet, even at school. They need to understand that advertisements are highly sophisticated and choreographed to help people remember a product and influence them to buy it.

*Captive Kids*, a report released by the nonprofit Consumers Union Educational Services in 1995, is based on data culled from eighteen months of observations in classrooms. Researchers examined the number and types of commercial messages at school.[2] Examples of commercialism in schools included book covers, bulletin boards, and signs on school buses paid for by advertisers, and in-school television programs that broadcast commercials. The report revealed that children are a lucrative market, spending about $73 billion per year of their own money and influencing the spending of $196 billion of their parents' money. Adding to the in-school barrage, students are also exposed to ads on the radio, on television, and increasingly, on-line.

Clearly, we need to equip students with the skills necessary to analyze and evaluate advertisements. The learning activities that follow provide multiple opportunities to develop critical thinking while honing language skills.

Preproduction

Since students at the Preproduction Stage mostly listen, this activity poses yes/no questions, uses simplified language, and utilizes print advertisements to help support understanding. It enables students to analyze print ads, make judgments, and classify them into groups.

Materials

Popular magazines with print advertisements; "Ad Search" activity sheet; scissors

Strategy

1. Distribute "Ad Search" activity sheets, scissors, and magazines to students [explain that "ad" is a shortened word for "advertisement"]. Point out the categories on the "Ad Search" sheet. Have them peruse the magazines, cutting out ads that correspond to each of the categories, and pasting them in the appropriate column. [You may want to have one already partially completed for demonstration/clarification purposes.]
2. After allowing students ample time to complete the "Ad Search" activity, lead a simple discussion using the following questioning strategy:
   a. For what type of product did you find the *most* number of advertisements?
   b. Which product had the *least* number of advertisements?
   c. Which advertisement did you like best?
   d. Do you have any of these products at home?

| Types of Products | Food | Medicine | Cosmetics | Clothing | Electronics |
|---|---|---|---|---|---|
| | | | | | |
| | | | | | |
| | | | | | |
| | | | | | |
| | | | | | |
| | | | | | |

# Television Commercials

## Early Production
In this activity, featuring the analysis of television commercials, dialogue will be facilitated by simple "who, what, where, and either/or" questions requiring one-word answers. This activity also helps students become accustomed to listening to English at normal speech speed, an important skill to develop.[3]

## Materials
Videotape of television commercials; VCR and TV monitor

## Strategy
1. Before class, videotape a variety of television commercials.
2. Have students watch each commercial.
3. Lead a class discussion by using the following questioning strategy after each commercial:
   a. What product is being sold?
   b. What is the advertiser promising or claiming? What does the advertiser say the product will do?
   c. To whom are they trying to sell?
   d. Do you think the information in the commercial is true? How could you find out? (Determine whether anyone in the class has used the product. If so, ask if the product is as good as the commercial claims.)
   e. (Explain that a "testimonial" is when a person speaks about a product s/he has used.) Were there any testimonials in the commercials?
   f. Why might commercials not always tell the truth?

# Marketing a Product

## Speech Emergence
Students whose English is at the level of Speech Emergence can speak in phrases and sentences, and can engage in group discussions provided there is teacher scaffolding. Teachers can begin to incorporate "how" and "why" questions and place students in supportive, cooperative learning groups.

## Materials
Full shampoo bottle, covered with plain paper or with label removed; drawing paper; colored pencils or markers

## Strategy
1. Display the plain bottle to students; ask them to pretend that it is a new shampoo that is not yet on the market. Ask: "Would you want to buy or use this shampoo? Why or why not?" (It is anticipated that most students will indicate that they will not purchase the product because it is unattractive, or there is not enough information, etc.)
2. Group students in pairs and tell them that they are to create the packaging for this new shampoo. Distribute drawing paper and colored pencils or markers, and ask each group to create a label that will make people want to buy the shampoo.
3. Display all the finished labels/bottles on a table at the conclusion of the activity. Have students compare and contrast their creations.
4. Questions to be discussed in pairs:
   a. Which shampoo label did you like best? Why?
   b. Which shampoo label would you not buy? Why?

# Radio and TV Commercials

## Intermediate Fluency
Because learners at the Intermediate Fluency stage can engage in extended and more complex dialogue, they are able to participate in more complex problem solving and writing activities. In this activity, students will create and produce their own commercials.

## Materials
Paper and pencil for brainstorming; optional: audiotaping or videotaping equipment

## Strategy
1. Decide whether you would like students to create a radio advertisement or a television commercial.
2. After placing students in small cooperative groups of no more than three, have them select a product for which they would like to create a commercial. (One possibility would be to extend the entrepreneurship lesson that follows and have students create a commercial advertising the proposed businesses developed in that lesson).
3. Inform students of the type of commercial they will be creating. Commercials produced for radio are typically no longer than sixty seconds; those for television are about thirty seconds long. Have them consider those qualities that are likely to get and retain the attention of their audiences.
4. Allow students to perform their commercials before the whole group. An alternate strategy would be to audiotape radio commercials and videotape TV ads; these tapes can then be played in class and discussed.

Speech Emergence/Intermediate Fluency

This modified game of bingo underscores the many global connections that may be present in the classroom. Within the familiar context of a bingo game, students are to obtain signatures from classmates in order to complete an entire row across, down, or diagonally.

## Materials

Class set of "International Bingo"; small prize (optional)

## Strategy

1. Distribute one game sheet ("International Bingo") to each student in class. Instruct students to sign their name in the center "free" box. All they will need for this activity is their pencil or pen. Explain that they are to collect classmates' signatures so that they complete an entire row (vertically, horizontally, or diagonally). To promote as much movement and interaction in the class as possible, a student may sign an individual classmate's game sheet only once. (As the teacher, you may or may not want to be available for signatures.) Make sure the students understand that afterwards they may be asked to explain why and how they were eligible to sign a particular box.
2. Allow enough time so that someone can collect enough signatures to achieve "bingo." When that occurs, give the signal for all students to take their seats. Check the winning game sheet aloud by calling out the names in each box and asking students to provide explanations as to why they were eligible to sign. You may want to award a small prize to the winner.
3. Bring closure to the activity by facilitating a discussion:
   a. How difficult was it to find signatures for the boxes?
   b. Which was the hardest box for which you had to find a signature?
   c. Which was the easiest?
   d. Did you learn something special about a classmate?

## Alternate Activity

You can devise your own International Bingo to suit individual units or regions of study, as an introductory activity to the subject. For example, if you are starting a unit on Latin America, you can design a bingo game with items such as "Have you or a family member ever visited South America?"; "Have you ever eaten Mexican food?"; "Can you name a sports star from Latin America?"; "Can you do a Latin American dance?"

# International Bingo

| | | | | |
|---|---|---|---|---|
| Have you ever traveled to another country? | Have you recently met someone from another country? | Are you wearing anything foreign-made? | Were you born in another country? | Do you have relatives in another country? |
| Can you name five countries in Africa? | Can you speak a language other than English? | Have you ever studied about another part of the world? | Do you have a Spanish surname? | Does your family own a car made in another country? |
| Are any part of your sneakers from another country? | Have you ever had a pen pal from another country? | "FREE" | Were you born in this state? | Can you name five countries in Latin America? |
| Is there a TV in your home made in another country? | Can you name five countries in Europe? | Do you enjoy foods from other cultures? | Have you ever traveled on an ocean liner? | Have you *never* met someone from another country? |
| Can you name five countries in Asia? | Can you greet someone in another language? | Have you ever traveled on an airplane? | Do you listen to music that comes from another country or culture? | Do you own a bike made in another country? |

# I'm a Global Consumer

In this activity, students analyze how many of the goods, clothing, food, and other items they consume and use daily are exports from other countries. To complete "I'm a Global Consumer," students find ten objects in their home that were made or otherwise imported from other countries.

Materials

"I'm a Global Consumer" worksheet; world map (wall or overhead transparency)

Strategy (Activity 1)

1. Assign the "I'm a Global Consumer" worksheet as homework the night before.
2. After students finish the sheet at home, lead a discussion in class using the following questions as springboards for discussion:
   a. Did the origin of any of the products surprise you? Where did you think the products were made?
   b. Why do you think that so many of our products come from other countries?
   c. Why do you think it is less expensive to import products than to produce them in our own country?
   d. What are the advantages of importing goods from another country? What are the disadvantages?
   e. Which countries show up most frequently on your list? Why do you think they do?

Name: _____

# I'm a Global Consumer

| Item | Company | Country(ies) |
|------|---------|--------------|
| 1. | | |
| 2. | | |
| 3. | | |
| 4. | | |
| 5. | | |
| 6. | | |
| 7. | | |
| 8. | | |
| 9. | | |
| 10. | | |

BONUS: Select one item from your list to bring to class and share with your classmates.

## I'm a Global Consumer
Strategy (Activity 2)

1. After having completed Activity 1 of this exercise, have students select and bring in one of the objects from their list to class. In pairs or small groups (mix ELL students and non-ELL students), allow students to share their objects. Then, a native speaker can report to the class for the group, stating:
   • what the objects are
   • what they are used for
   • where they were made

2. As students disclose the place of origin of each object, note its location on a wall map or transparency, creating a class composite. After all students have shared their artifacts, lead a discussion regarding our global economy using the composite map:
   a. Who makes what we own?
   b. Why are so many things made in other countries?
   c. How do we benefit from the global economy?
   d. What problems come with being part of the global economy?

# Entrepreneurship: Creating Your Own Business

Entrepreneurs are those who create, organize, and assume the risk of a business; successful entrepreneurs are often innovative, flexible, confident, disciplined, and persistent. A business is an organization involved in producing a good or service with the intent of making a profit for the owner.

Because the entrepreneur often has to undertake a large financial risk, not all businesspeople are well-suited to be true entrepreneurs. New businesses have a high rate of failure. In the activities that follow, students will consider basic marketplace issues that entrepreneurs must consider before starting a business. They will also develop a basic understanding of consumer needs and the intricacies involved in starting a new enterprise by designing a business plan. Two particularly useful resources are the website Young Biz (http://www.youngbiz.com) and the print resource *Young Biz Magazine*. Both resources provide information for and by young people who have started their own businesses.

## Materials
Pictures of businesses that sell goods or products (clipped from magazines or sale circulars) mounted on numbered index cards

## Strategy
1. Distribute a set of five cards to each student.
2. Have these instructions written on the board: What does each business sell? Number your own paper, and draw a picture of what each business sells students. Which businesses are where you live?
   NOTE: The teacher can label each business card on the board and ask the students to copy the name on their papers.

## Early Production
### Materials
Chalk/dry erase board

### Strategy
1. Lead a class discussion by using the following questioning strategy:
   a. List ten businesses in your community.
   b. What do these businesses sell?
2. Make two columns on the board: one for businesses that sell products or goods, one for businesses that provide a service.
3. Which businesses sell only one type of goods and services? Which sell more than one?
   Use symbols on board: "<1" for first question; ">1" for second question. [Explain "greater than" and "less than" signs if necessary.]
4. Ask students: In your opinion, is it better to sell more than one thing? Or is it better to focus on just one?

Extension Activity

In small groups, have non-ELL students ask each other the following questions and then paraphrase, if needed, for the ELL students:

1. Can you think of a product that almost everyone uses today that did not exist when your parents were your age?
2. Can you think of a business that existed 50 or 100 years ago that no longer exists?
3. What are some jobs that existed in the early 1900s that are no longer needed?
4. What are some jobs today that did not exist in your parents' or your grandparents' time?
5. What are some jobs that have been in existence for at least 100 years?
6. Can you think of a toy or game that your parent or grandparent played with that is still sold today?
7. Can you think of a business that is needed in your community or neighborhood but does not yet exist?
8. Why do you think this business would do well (have customers)?

## Speech Emergence

Although part of the American Dream has been to own one's own business, the statistics for new business ventures reveal that more than half of new businesses fail within the first ten years. Often, the failure can be traced to poor planning. Prospective business owners need to research the industry, their competition, and their intended market. In this exercise, students will identify a good or service they think would make a good business, consider the market and competition, and write a brief rationale and business description.

Materials

"My New Business" handout; teacher-made handout with local business examples and pictures

Strategy

1. You can either start where the previous (Early Production) activity left off, or you can start fresh, with students brainstorming about potential businesses. A teacher-made handout with pictures of local businesses would be helpful for ELL and non-ELL students alike.
2. Place students in cooperative learning groups of two or three. Have them decide on one good or service that they would like to develop a business around.
3. Distribute the handout, "My New Business." Instruct students to answer all questions and draft a business description.
4. After allowing sufficient time to complete the work, have small groups share it with the entire class.

## Intermediate Fluency

Each year, investors look over hundreds of business plans. However, each investor may only invest in two or three. Using the rationale for a business that was created in the preceding activity, students will research their proposed businesses and prepare a presentation for prospective investors.

### Materials
The handout, "My New Business: Business Plan."

### Strategy
1. Using the handout "My New Business: Business Plan," students are to provide a detailed description of their proposed businesses to potential investors. (Note: ELL students can use bullets with short phrases rather than write out a response in paragraph form.)
2. After students have completed the handout, have them create a presentation for prospective investors (their classmates will serve as potential venture capitalists). Inform them that they can use multimedia (pictures, music, handouts, *PowerPoint*, etc.) or any other format they think would catch people's attention.
3. Have small groups "sell" their businesses to potential investors (role-played by their classmates). Explain how the investors will get their money—and more—back. Encourage the investors to ask questions at the end of each presentation.
4. Optional: Have investors indicate on anonymous ballots whether they would invest in the businesses presented. Why or why not? This information can also be given to the business owners as feedback on their business plans.

---

"Business Plan" answer key
1. product, service
2. competition
3. need, grow
4. customers
5. name?
6. description, function, operate

---

# My New Business
Business Plan

Instructions: Fill in the blanks using words from the word bank below. Then, answer the questions based on your proposed business.

| | |
|---|---|
| description | function |
| product | operate |
| grow | service |
| business | competition |
| name | customers |
| need | |

1. What _____ or _____ do you think would make a good business?

   _____

   _____

2. What _____ already exists?

   _____

   _____

3. Do you have any evidence that _____ for this product or service will continue to_____ ?

   _____

   _____

4. Who would be your main _____ ?

   _____

   _____

5. What will be your business's_____ ?

   _____

6. On the back of this paper, write a brief _____ of your proposed business and how it will _____ or_____ :

# Living Within Your Means: Budgeting

Since no one has unlimited wealth, being a participant in the economy requires that people make choices based on limited resources. People must choose certain things, while giving up others. All students must learn the importance of living within their means when making both short-term and long-term economic decisions. At its very simplest, a budget takes into consideration income and expenditures. These budgeting activities will offer the students experience in making thoughtful decisions based on the amount of money that is available to them.

## Preproduction
### What Money Will Buy
This activity will allow the students to become familiar with products that are available to consumers, while at the same time practicing solving math problems and building vocabulary words. [Since numbers are the same in any language, this allows students in the beginning stages of language acquisition to work with concepts that are familiar to them.]

### Materials
Sale circular from a local grocery store; simulated money; calculator (optional)

### Strategy
1. Create one simulated bill each in the denominations of $1, $5, $10, and $20.
2. Using the sale circular from a grocery store, have students identify items listed in the circular that they are able to purchase with a single bill. Can you buy _____?
3. After the students have found single items that they can afford using one bill, allow them to find multiple products using the larger denomination bills. Can the student purchase enough food for dinner for one with $5? $10?

## Early Production
### Eating Out
Using restaurant menus, students try to feed a family of four based on limited resources. They will analyze restaurant offerings, costs, and be forced to make choices to stay within budget.

### Materials
Several paper menus from local restaurants; calculator

### Strategy
1. Explain to the students that they have $50 with which to purchase a meal at a restaurant for a family of four (two adults and two children). The students are to peruse each menu and choose one restaurant from which to purchase their meals. They are to keep a tab of the cost of each item and calculate the total.
2. Afterwards, lead a discussion by asking:
   a. What will you eat as your entrée? What will you drink? Will you have dessert?
   b. Did you choose a restaurant that offers children's meals? Why?
   c. Remember that if you choose a "sit-down" restaurant, you must leave a gratuity (usually 15 percent or 20 percent). What's the advantage of eating at a "serve-yourself" restaurant?

Speech Emergence
**Getting A Used Car**

Materials

*AutoTrader* magazine, or any sales circular that lists used automobiles (alternatively, if the classroom has an Internet connection, a simple search using the keywords "used vehicles" will provide sources, with pictures, of vehicles for sale)

Strategy

1. Explain to the students that they are each going to purchase a used vehicle. Explain that they each have $5,000 with which to purchase a vehicle.

2. Show the students copies of the *AutoTrader* magazine, or allow students to look up used vehicles on the Internet. Have them identify three vehicles under or close to $5,000.

3. Explain to the students that several factors besides price should influence their decisions on whether or not to purchase certain vehicles. Besides price, a prospective buyer should weigh vehicle features with intended use. For example, smaller cars and engines get better gas mileage, but because of their size, cannot transport as many people comfortably. Students may also want to take into consideration whether automobiles are made within the United States or are imported from other countries.

4. After students have selected their vehicles, they should be able to tell the other students and the teacher why they made the choices that they did. Examples of answers could include: "The Honda has a four-cylinder engine. This will get better gas mileage. A four-door car will let me take my friends along with me."

5. After the students have "purchased" their vehicles, the teacher can show them the *Kelly Blue Book* value of the vehicles (available online at www.kbb.com) to see if the students paid what the vehicles were worth. This activity enables students to make a realistic economic choice, similar to what they will be faced with when they are adults. Students can check to see how "smart" their decisions were, based on the accepted market value of each vehicle.

Intermediate Fluency

## Just Out of College

By creating a budget worksheet, students are forced to make choices about how they want to live and to simulate the budgeting they will do as adults. They will differentiate between economic needs and wants and consider that all economic decisions have advantages and disadvantages.

Materials

"Budget Worksheet"

Strategy

1. Explain to the students that they are to assume the role of someone who has just graduated from college. They have started a new job and will be making a net income of $2,000 per month.
2. Show the students the "Budget Worksheet," and inform them that they will have to make decisions regarding their lifestyles. Encourage the students to consider the advantages and disadvantages associated with the decisions that they will make.
3. After the students have completed the worksheet, ask them to answer the questions at the end of the budget worksheet and be prepared to discuss them with the rest of the class.
4. Conclude the class by asking the following questions:
   a. Did you realize how much money is required to live on your own?
   b. Did any of the expenses surprise you? Why?
   c. Are any other expenses a part of your lifestyle? What are they?
   d. How much money do you have left at the end of the month after all the bills are paid?
   Note: This lesson might also provide a springboard for a discussion of cultural differences about living with parents versus living on one's own.

# Budget Worksheet

At its simplest, a budget is a plan that helps you make decisions about your needs and wants based on your income. Pretend you have just graduated and are making $2,000 per month at your new job. You need to make some decisions about how and where you are going to live. For each category, circle a lifestyle choice:

## Rent
Live in an apartment with a roommate
$250 per month

Live at home with parents
$100 per month

## Automobile
New car
$200 monthly payments
$150 per month in auto insurance
$75 per month for gas

Drive used car parents give you
$100 per month in repair costs
$100 per month in auto insurance
$90 per month for gas

## Food/Groceries
Buy your own food
$200 per month

Live at home with parents
$100 per month

## Utilities
Telephone $30 per month
Utilities $125 per month

Telephone $10 per month
Utilities $50 per month

## Medical/Health Insurance
Individual Coverage
$180 per month

Under family's coverage
$50 per month

## Clothing
Limited, living on your own
$80 per month

More expendable income
$150 per month

## Entertainment
Limited, living on your own
$50 per month

More expendable income
$100 per month

## Savings
Limited, living on your own
$50 per month

More expendable income
$150 per month

## Incidentals/Miscellaneous
Limited, living on your own
$80 per month

More expendable income
$160 per month

TOTAL: _____

TOTAL: _____

Today, more than ever, the United States is part of a complex international economic system. All countries specialize in some goods and services that they sell to other countries, on which they are dependent for other goods and services. ELL students may be intrinsically interested in the international marketplace since many of them are likely to be immigrants themselves. All students will benefit from understanding how global trade impacts their communities.

### Preproduction
### Materials
A varied collection of products made in various countries; "Where in the World...?" activity sheet; wall map of world

### Strategy
1. Display products prominently on table, accessible to all.
2. Have students fill out the activity sheet, "Where in the World...?", explaining that they will classify products by their origins. Point to each area on a wall map while explaining the chart. They are to examine each product and determine from which continent it came, filling out the sheet as they go. Students can work individually or in pairs.
3. After students have had an opportunity to complete the activity sheet, lead a class discussion:
   a. Which continent made the most products?
   b. Which continent made the least products?
   c. How many products are made in _____?

# "Where in the World...?"

| Africa | Asia | North America | Europe | Central & South America |
|--------|------|---------------|--------|-------------------------|
|        |      |               |        |                         |
|        |      |               |        |                         |
|        |      |               |        |                         |
|        |      |               |        |                         |
|        |      |               |        |                         |

**International Trade**

Early Production

Materials

"I'm a Global Consumer" worksheet (p. 90); world map; push pins

Strategy

1. Have students find ten items in their homes, completing the worksheet "I'm a Global Consumer." Have them select one item appropriate to bring to school and share in class.
2. Share lists and items brought from home in class.
3. Using a world map tacked onto a bulletin board, push pins (or some other colored marker) into the locations identified by the students in the home exercise.
4. Lead a class discussion using the following questioning strategy:
   a. Which country has the most pins?
   b. What *types* of things does that country produce most (food, clothes, electronics)?
   c. Which countries have *no* pins?

# The Global Parking Lot

## Early Production

This learning activity enables students to consider the impact of international trade on their community by examining one product: automobiles. Kinesthetic learners will especially appreciate the physical nature of this activity. Using the faculty parking lot, students analyze the country of origin of the cars, plot the data, and calculate percentages. Students will compare and contrast the number of foreign and domestic vehicles in their community while developing data-gathering skills, graphing skills, and practicing basic math computations.

## Materials

The Global Parking Lot Data Gathering Sheet; clipboards (optional); pencils; graphing paper

## Strategy

1. Group students in pairs. Distribute one copy of the Global Parking Lot Data Gathering Sheet to each pair along with a clipboard, if used.
2. Tell students that they are going to gather data about which cars are represented in the school's faculty parking lot. They are to record their findings with tally marks on the Data Gathering Sheet. (Using the board, explain and show how to use tally marks, using a different example.) If a make of car is not on the Data Gathering Sheet, instruct students to record the car make at the bottom. (Later they can research the manufacturer and add to the appropriate category.)
3. Escort students to the parking lot and have them record their findings.
4. After returning to class, allow students time to research the country of origin of each of the car manufacturers and complete the sheet.
5. In pairs, have students plot the data on the graphing paper and answer the questions. (These data can be graphed in a number of ways; bar graphs would work well.)
6. Have student pairs share their findings and responses with the whole class.

## Extension Activity

Have students research the cars on the Internet, in terms of price, number sold per year in the U.S., reliability (e.g., Consumer Reports), safety (e.g., Insurance Safety Board), etc.

# The Global Parking Lot
Data Gathering Sheet

| Car Make/Manufacturer | Number | Country of Origin |
|---|---|---|
| Ford | | |
| Chrysler | | |
| Chevrolet | | |
| Pontiac | | |
| Saturn | | |
| Cadillac | | |
| Other General Motors Cars | | |
| Mercedes-Benz | | |
| Saab | | |
| Nissan | | |
| Toyota | | |
| Honda | | |
| Volkswagen | | |
| Acura | | |
| Other Foreign | | |
| Other Domestic | | |

Unknown: _____

_____

# The Global Parking Lot

## Questions
(Use graph paper to demonstrate your answer)

1. Which type of car did you see the most in the parking lot?

2. Which type of car did you see the least?

3. Which country produces the most cars used by your school's teachers?

4. Which country produces the least number of cars used by your school's teachers?

5. Which car would you choose? Why?

## Notes

1. National Council on Economic Education (NCEE), *The Standards in Economics Survey* (New York: NCEE, 2001).

2. Consumers Union Educational Services (CUES), *Captive Kids: A Report on Commercial Pressures on Kids at* Schools (New York: CUES, 1995).

3. Joseph A. Wipf, "Shortwave Radio and the Second Language Class," *Modern Language Journal* 68 no. 1 (1984): 7-12.

---

## Learned Societies and Useful Economic Education Websites

Cool Bank
http://www.coolbank.com/

Consumer Education for Teens
http://www.wa.gov/ago/youth

Economic Education Station
http://web.centre.edu/~econed/

Economic Education Web
http://ecedweb.unomaha.edu/

Economic Literacy Project
http://woodrow.mpls.frb.fed.us/sylloge/econlit/more-
    resources.html

Federal Reserve
http://www.federalreserveeducation.org/

Foundation for Teaching Economics
http://www.fte.org

It All Adds Up
http://www.italladdsup.org

Kids' Almanac: Business and Technology
http://www.yahooligans.com/content/ka/index.html

Kids' Money
http://www.kidsmoney.org/

Northwestern Mutual's "The Mint"
http://www.themint.org

National Association of Economic Educators
http://ecedweb.unomaha.edu/naee/naeepamp.htm

National Center for Research in Economic Education
http://www.cba.unl.edu/additional/econed/ncree.html

National Council on Economic Education
http://www.ncee.net

A Pedestrian's Guide to the Economy
http://www.amosweb.com

Teenpreneurs Club
http://www.blackenterprise.com/S0/PageOpen.asp?Source
    =Articles/DEFAULT.htm

Understanding USA
http://www.understandingusa.com

U.S. Treasury Department
http://www.treas.gov

Young Biz
http://www.youngbiz.com

Youth Link
http://www.ssa.gov/kids/index.htm

# Part 3

# Internet Resources

# CHAPTER 10

# Professional Organizations and Resources on the Internet

The following websites will assist teachers in learning more about the special needs of language minority students and in adapting existing lessons for them.

## Lesson Planning, Learning Activities, and Printable Materials

Boggle's World
http://bogglesworld.com/
*Comprehensive resource site offering lesson plans, worksheets, flash cards, game boards, and discussion forums.*

Center for Applied Linguistics
http://www.cal.org
*The CAL website provides detailed analyses of language issues and provides links to language-related databases, clearinghouses, and centers.*

CESOL
http://literacytech.worlded.org/docs/cesol/links.htm
*Computers and English for Speakers of Other Languages is a gateway site to lessons, teacher resources, software and links to other useful sites.*

Dave's ESOL Café
http://www.eslcafe.com
*Billed as "The Internet's Meeting Place for ESL/EFL Students and Teachers from Around the World!", this easy-to-navigate site offers many resources for both students and teachers.*

Digital Education Network
http://www.go-ed.com/elt
*This comprehensive site offers teaching advice, instructional materials, and student resources.*

English as a Second Language
http://www.kings.k12.ca.us/kcoe/curric/esl.html
*Gateway site for ESL resources.*

English Learning Fun Site
http://www.elfs.com
*Enjoyable activities for English Language Learners that include conversation, accent reduction, idioms and slang terms.*

ESL Lounge
www.esl-lounge.com
*Excellent teachers' site loaded with lesson plans, worksheets, teaching tips, and more.*

ESL Party Land
http://www.eslpartyland.com
*Students can access interactive quizzes and activities, discussion forums and a chat room, and many links. Teachers will find useful lesson plans, reproducible materials, discussion forums and a chat room, employment postings, and links.*

Internet for ESL Teachers
http://edvista.com/claire/internet-esl.html
*This gateway site includes links to organizations, teaching tools, and professional articles.*

Kenji Hakuta's Website
http://www.stanford.edu/~hakuta/
*This Stanford University professor's website provides valuable information, discussion of research policy, and answers critical questions for teachers of English language learners.*

National Clearinghouse for Bilingual Education
http://www.ncbe.gwu.edu
*NCBE's site is linked to dozens of resources to help teachers and schools deliver effective education to linguistically and culturally diverse learners.*

Selected Links for ESL & EFL Students
http://iteslj.org/ESL.html
*Maintained by the Internet TESL Journal, these sites were selected for their ease of navigation, lack of advertising, and utility for students.*

TESL/FL Resource Guide
http://www.tesol.net/mele.faq.html
*Includes a discussion of important terminology, identifies useful resources including websites, print materials, software, and teachers' aids.*

## Centers, Organizations, and Government Offices

American Council on the Teaching of Foreign Languages (ACTFL)
http://www.actfl.org
*National organization "dedicated to the improvement and expansion of the teaching and learning of all languages at all levels of instruction." Includes links to publications, standards, and information about upcoming workshops.*

Center for Applied Linguistics
http://www.cal.org
*Comprehensive site featuring research, teaching materials, and details of ongoing projects for ESOL, Foreign Language and Linguistics.*

Center for Multilingual Multicultural Research
http://www.usc.edu/dept/education/CMMR
*This University of Southern California website provides indices of print, audio-visual, and technology resources as well as links to dozens of other useful websites.*

Center for Research on Education, Diversity, and Excellence (CREDE)
http://www.cal.org/crede/
*This national research center seeks to "identify and develop effective educational practices for linguistic and cultural minority students." The website serves as a portal to research and publications as well as descriptions and contact information of successful programs.*

National Association for Bilingual Education (NABE)
http://www.nabe.org
*The website of this national organization, concerned with the education of language minority students in the U.S., features "frequently asked questions," information about parents' rights, print materials, and links to other resources.*

National Clearinghouse for English Language Acquisition
http://www.ncela.gwu.edu
*Formerly the National Clearinghouse for Bilingual Education (NCBE), the NCELA is funded by the U.S. Department of Education. Among the many useful features, this site provides demographics of ELL students, information about promoting cultural understanding, and links to bulletins and state resources.*

The Office of English Language Acquisition, Language Enhancement, and Academic Achievement for Limited English Proficient Students (OELA)
http://www.ed.gov/offices/OBEMLA
*National U.S. government office whose mission it is to promote high quality education for ELLs through school and program reform.*

Project ESOL Tapestry
http://www.coedu.usf.edu/esol/project_esol_tapestry.htm
*A project at the University of South Florida designed to improve curriculum and instruction for ELL students via a research community, web-based learning, and the development of technology-enhanced resources.*

Teachers of English to Speakers of Other Languages
http://www.tesol.org
*The largest membership organization for ESOL teachers, this site boasts career information, educational links, and opportunities to network with other educators.*

U.S. Deptartment of Education, Office for Civil Rights: Programs for English Language Learners
http://www.ed.gov/offices/OCR/ELL/
*This government site provides an overview of ELL programs, resource materials for developing a program, and program evaluation guidelines.*

## Standards

ESL Standards for Pre-K–12 Students
http://www.tesol.org/assoc/k12standards/it/01.html

ESOL Performance Standards
http://www.coedu.usf.edu/esol/tapestry/esol_performance_standards.htm

NCSS Curriculum Standards for Social Studies
http://www.socialstudies.org/standards

Office of Multicultural Student Language Education
http://www.firn.edu/doe/bin00011/perstand.htm

Standards for Foreign Language Learning
http://www.actfl.org

TESOL/NCATE Standards for the Accreditation of Initial Programs in P-12 ESL Teacher Education
http://www.ncate.org/standard/new%20program%20standards/tesol.pdf

# Glossary of Terms

Please note: Definitions of terms marked with an asterisk (*) are from the *Longman Dictionary of Language Teaching and Applied Linguistics*[1]

**American Council on the Teaching of Foreign Languages (ACTFL)**—the national professional organization for foreign language teachers.

**acculturation**—the process of becoming familiar with and competent in a second (or third, etc.) culture without losing the native culture. Acculturation is contrasted with assimilation (see below).

**assimilation**—the process of becoming familiar with and competent in a second (or third, etc.) culture through the abandonment of the native culture and the adoption of the second culture's practices and values.

**Basic Interpersonal Communication Skills (BICS)**—language used for social communication that typically takes approximately two years to develop. BICS is contrasted with CALP (see below).

**\*Bilingual Education**—the use of a second or foreign language for teaching content. There are different approaches, which include: (a) immersion—the use of one language in schooling which is not the student's native language;(b) maintenance—the use of the student's native language upon entrance into the program followed by a gradual change to the use of the second language for teaching some subjects and the native language for teaching others; (c) transitional—use of the student's native language upon entering school, followed by the eventual use of the school language only.

**Bilingual support**—assistance offered in a person's native language to support comprehension and expression in the second language

**C1, C2**—C1 is an individual's first culture and C2 is the individual's second culture; these are analogous to first and second languages (L1 and L2).

**Cognitive Academic Language Learning Approach (CALLA)**—an approach to teaching that focuses on teaching subject content to develop students' English proficiency. It includes three emphases: (a) content-based instruction; (b) academic language development; and (c) learning strategy instruction.

**Cognitive Academic Language Proficiency (CALP)**—academic language required to succeed in school. Tasks that require CALP typically lack contextual support and are relatively cognitively demanding. It takes approximately a minimum of five to seven years to develop CALP.

**cognitive complexity**—the degree to which a task is cognitively easy or difficult for the student attempting it.

**comprehension checks**—attempts to ascertain whether an ELL student has comprehended some form of communication or instruction, usually in the form of questions or tasks.

**Computer-Assisted Language Learning (CALL)**—using a computer to teach second or foreign languages. CALL encompasses computer-based or computer-enhanced instruction.

**content-based instruction**—teaching a second or foreign language through academic content rather than focusing solely on language and its properties.

**contextual support**—extralinguistic cues, such as visuals, props, or hands-on experiences that enable comprehension through means other than language.

**conversational English**—informal English used for communicating with friends, peers, or others.

**\*cross-cultural communication**—exchanging information between persons from different cultural backgrounds.

**cross-cultural simulations**—teaching techniques that place students in a simulated cultural environment that is foreign to them or that requires students to interact with others who take on cultural characteristics different from their own.

**culture assimilators**—a brief description of a cultural dilemma, presented from the perspective of the culture of focus, with three or four choices of how to solve the dilemma or on how to explain the cultural reasons for the dilemma. Students must select the culturally appropriate solution or explanation. The choices range from unacceptable in that culture to optimal.

**culture capsules**—an instructional activity that presents features of a different culture in a brief, interesting fashion.

**Direct Reading Thinking Activity (DR-TA)**—a learning strategy in which students make predictions on a topic and then read the topic.

**discourse rich**—an activity that requires discussion and interchange.

**dual language or two-way bilingual programs**—a bilingual education approach that places language minority and language majority students together in a school and offers part of the instructional day in both languages for students (e.g., ELL students spend part of their day learning in their native language and part of their day learning in English, and students who are native speakers of English spend part of their day learning in English and part of their day learning in the first language of the ELL students). This approach enables both English language learners and students who are native speakers of English to become bilingual.

**Early Production**—the second stage of the Natural Approach. Students can form one or two-word responses at this stage.

**ELL/English Language Learners (ELLs)**—non-native speakers who are learning English.

**English as an Additional Language (EAL)**—a less common alternative to ESL or ESOL.

**English as a Foreign Language (EFL)**—teaching English in countries/locations where it is not the first language of the majority of the population.

**English as a New Language (ENL)**—an alternative to ESL or ESOL.

**English as a Second Language (ESL)**—term used primarily in post-secondary settings to describe the subject of teaching English to non-native speakers residing in a location where English is the first language of the majority of the population.

**English for Academic Purposes (EAP)**—English study that focuses on developing academic language.

**English for Speakers of Other Languages (ESOL)**—a popular acronym describing the subject when it is taught in K-12 schools.

**English for Specific Purposes (ESP)**—English study that focuses on the specialized vocabulary of a particular trade or subject area.

**expressive vocabulary**—vocabulary used in speaking or writing. See productive skills.

**\*first language (L1)**—a person's language which was acquired first.

**\*fluency**—the degree of proficiency in communication including the ability to write or speak with ease.

**\*formulaic chunks of language**—language segments comprised of several words learned together and used as if they were a single item. For example, *How ya doin?*

**heritage language maintenance**—a goal of certain types of bilingual education, which is to avoid the loss of the first language as the student becomes more proficient in English.

**home language**—the language spoken in the student's home, often used synonymously with heritage language.

***immersion**—a type of bilingual education where students who speak only one language enter a school where a different language is used for instruction for everyone. If the students are taught in the different language all day, it is called a total immersion program, but if they are taught in a different language for part of the day, it is called a partial immersion program. See *Submersion* also.

**Intermediate Fluency**—the fourth stage of the Natural Approach. Students have acquired BICS and are developing CALP at this stage.

**L1, L2**—see first language, second language.

**Language Experience Approach (LEA)**—after sharing an experience, students express themselves in their own words while the teacher or a more proficient peer writes these words down. Students then build a polished text from their own verbal expression.

**language majority student**—a student whose first language is the language spoken by the majority of people in the country where the school is located (e.g., English in the U.S.).

**language minority student**—a student whose first language is not the majority language of the country where the school is located (e.g., English in the U.S.) and who may or may not be fully proficient in the majority language.

**Limited English Proficient (LEP)**—a federal term for a student who is not a native speaker of English, has not developed full proficiency in the language and requires support services (i.e., ESOL classes or modified instruction in content classes) and monitoring.

**mainstreaming**—placement of English language learners into regular classrooms (with native speakers of English) for the learning of content.

***metalinguistic knowledge**—knowledge of the forms and structure of a language developed through analyzing the language.

**modified input**—altering the way that information is conveyed, including simplifying language, gesturing, or providing visual cues.

**modified interaction**—altering the way that information is exchanged, including checking for comprehension, re-stating and paraphrasing each other's utterances, or asking for clarification.

***monolingual**—someone who knows and uses only one language.

**National Association for Bilingual Education (NABE)**—the national professional organization for bilingual educators.

**Natural Approach**—an approach to teaching English language learners that emphasizes successful communication; this approach segments the process of second language acquisition into four basic levels and details student and teacher behaviors at each one.

**negotiate meaning/negotiation of meaning**—the back-and-forth process of asking for clarification or verification through questions, rephrasing, etc., to ensure understanding of the communication.

**Potential English Proficient (PEP)**—sometimes used as an alternative to LEP to avoid the notion of limitations.

**Preproduction**—the first stage of the Natural Approach. Students at this stage can comprehend contextualized simple language and respond non-verbally.

**productive skills**—speaking and writing, also called active skills.

***proficiency**—skill in using a language for a specific purpose.

**realia**—real objects, props, and hands-on materials used in teaching or learning.

**receptive skills**—listening and reading, also called passive skills.

**SDAIE model (Specially Designed Academic Instruction in English)**—a technique that focuses on the lesson content, comprehension strategies, connections with the ELL students' own experiences, and classroom interaction.

**SQ4R (Survey, Question, Read, Reflect, Recite, and Review)**—a technique to help students comprehend reading texts.

***Second Language (L2)**—a native language in a country learned by those with another first language.

***second language acquisition (SLA)**—the process of developing proficiency in a second or foreign language.

**second language learning**—a term that can be synonymous with SLA, but in some contexts may refer more to the formal study of language in school.

***Sheltered ESOL instruction**—an approach to teaching English language learners separately in which content is taught in English and made comprehensible by special instructional techniques. It aims to enable ELL students to acquire high levels of English proficiency while achieving in the content areas, i.e., to teach academic subjects and language simultaneously until the student is ready for mainstreaming.

**Silent Period**—an early stage in second language acquisition that many students experience. During this time, students can comprehend much more than they can express, and studies have shown that allowing students time (weeks or even months) to listen before requiring them to speak or repeat can be beneficial.

**Speech Emergence**—the third stage of the Natural Approach. Students at this stage can utter simple phrases.

***Submersion**—placing English language learners into regular classrooms with native speakers without special assistance in English. Few accommodations are made for these students' special needs. See also *Immersion*.

***syntax**—how words combine to form sentences and the rules for forming sentences.

**TPR (Total Physical Response)**—A teaching method developed by James Asher that is especially effective during the silent period or preproduction stage. Students demonstrate comprehension by following commands, such as "stand up" or "raise your right hand."

**Teach the Text Backward**—a technique to help ELL students be better prepared before actually reading a text.

**Teachers of English to Speakers of Other Languages (TESOL)**—the international professional organization for teachers of ESOL. It is also the term used in the United States for Teaching English to Speakers of Other Languages, which is called English Language Teaching (ELT) in Great Britain.

**V.I.P.S (Voice, Intonation, Pausing, and Speed)**—a technique to help teachers remember to modify their speech when speaking with ELL students so as to improve communication.

***whole language approach**—an approach to first and second language teaching based on the following principles: (a) language is presented as a whole and not as isolated parts; (b) learning activities move from whole to part, rather than from part to whole; (c) listening, speaking, reading, and writing are used; (d) language is learned through social interaction.

**Note**
1. Jack C. Richards, John Platt and Heidi Platt, *Longman Dictionary of Language Teaching and Applied Linguistics* (Essex, U.K.: Longman Group UK Ltd., 1992).

# About the Authors

**Bárbara C. Cruz** is Associate Professor in the social science education program of the College of Education at the University of South Florida (USF), Tampa. Born in Havana, Cuba, she was herself an ELL student in several U.S. public schools. Dr. Cruz's teaching and research interests include multicultural and global perspectives in education, minority issues and diversity in education, and innovative strategies for teaching social studies. She has facilitated teacher workshops for numerous school systems and frequently receives invitations to be a guest speaker from international and national professional organizations. She is the author of journal articles, curriculum guides for teachers, and an adolescent biography series on inspirational Hispanics.

**Joyce W. Nutta** is an Associate Professor of Foreign/Second Language Education in the College of Education at the University of South Florida (USF), Tampa. She holds a Ph.D. in Second Language Acquisition, a master's degree in Applied Linguistics, and a bachelor's degree in Mass Communications. She has conducted teacher training on multicultural issues throughout the state of Florida, and has received many awards for her teaching, community involvement, research, and management of grant-funded projects. She has written and directed fifteen grants from a variety of funding sources. Dr. Nutta's research interests include integrating ESOL into teacher preparation programs, computer-assisted language learning (CALL), and distance learning. Prior to her current position at USF, she served as coordinator of the adult English for Speakers of Other Languages Program for Pinellas County Schools, where she taught ESOL and Italian, among other subjects.

**Jason O'Brien** teaches fifth grade at Sacred Heart Academy in Tampa, Florida. He is also a doctoral student at the University of South Florida, majoring in Curriculum and Instruction, with an emphasis in social studies and a cognate area of teaching English to Speakers of Other Languages. He is also an Adjunct Professor at USF where he teaches social studies teaching methods. His research interests include multicultural education, diversity issues, and Latin American and Caribbean studies.

**Carine M. Feyten** is Professor of Foreign Language Education in the College of Education and Chair of the Department of Secondary Education at the University of South Florida (USF) in Tampa. Originally from Belgium, she is fluent in five languages and has won several teaching and research awards. Since 1986 she has been extensively involved in teacher training and inservice training both in foreign languages and ESOL in the state of Florida. She has taught a variety of ESOL courses including applied linguistics, cross-cultural awareness, methods, and ESOL strategies for content-area teachers. Dr. Feyten has presented a number of conference papers and published several articles in the areas of listening, applied linguistics, cross-cultural communication, and language learning/teaching. Her current interests are very much tied to the integration of technology in education and more specifically to the concept of virtual instruction. She is editor and author of works in the field, such as *Virtual Instruction: Issues and Insights from an International Perspective* and *Teaching ESL/EFL with the Internet: Catching the Wave.*

**Jane M. Govoni** is an Assistant Professor in the Education Department at Saint Leo University, which is located about 25 miles north of Tampa, Florida. She holds a Ph.D. in Curriculum and Instruction with an emphasis in Second Language Acquisition, and an M.A. in Spanish from Boston College. Dr. Govoni has taught Spanish from K-16 as well as ESOL to international graduate students. She is presently coordinator of the ESOL Program at Saint Leo University. She was senior reviewer of the textbook series "En Español" and has published articles on teacher training, distance learning, and ESOL in teacher preparation programs. Currently she is a recipient of a Service Learning Grant, and is seeking other grants in this field to foster the promotion of community and academic service and the mission and core values at Saint Leo.

# Index

tomato 56
tomato sauce 55
Toyota 104
Triangle Shirtwaist Factory 44–49
Trinidad and Tobago 75
Tubman, Harriet 40
Tunisia 75
Turkey 75
typewriter 58

## U

U.S. Bureau of the Census 42
U.S. Department of Education 3
U.S. Government Printing Office (GPO) 71
U.S. House of Representatives 71
U.S. Senate 71
Uganda 76
United Kingdom 75
United States Census 2000 4
United States History 39–50
Uruguay 75
USSR 75

## V

Venezuela 9, 75
Vietnam 3, 13, 75
Vietnamese 10, 12, 14
Vietnam War 39
Volkswagen 104
Volta, Alessandro 58

## W

Wagner, Robert 49
Washington, George 40
Watt, James 58
wheat 56
Whitney, Eli 58
wireless telegraph/radio 58
women's suffrage 72–76
Word of the Week 32
world history 51–61
Worth, Edward 48

## X

x-rays 58

## Y

Yemen Arab Republic 76
*Young Biz Magazine* 92
Yugoslavia 75

## Z

Zaire 76

JEROME LIBRARY
CURRICULUM RESOURCE CENTER
BOWLING GREEN STATE UNIVERSITY
BOWLING GREEN, OHIO 43403

## DATE DUE

SEP 2 1 2010

GAYLORD

PRINTED IN U.S.A.

CURR 300.71 P29

Passport to learning